The North American Fourth Edition

Cambridge Latin Course

Unit 3

Omnibus Workbook

REVISION TEAM

Stephanie M. Pope, Chair
Norfolk Academy, Norfolk, Virginia

Patricia E. Bell
formerly of Centennial Collegiate and Vocational Institute, Guelph, Ontario, Canada

Stan Farrow
formerly of the David and Mary Thomson Collegiate Institute, Scarborough, Ontario, Canada

Richard M. Popeck
Stuarts Draft High School and Stuarts Draft Middle School, Stuarts Draft, Virginia

Anne Shaw
Lawrence High School and Lawrence Free State High School, Lawrence, Kansas

**CAMBRIDGE**
UNIVERSITY PRESS

CAMBRIDGE UNIVERSITY PRESS
Cambridge, New York, Melbourne, Madrid, Cape Town,
Singapore, São Paulo, Delhi, Tokyo, Mexico City

Cambridge University Press
32 Avenue of the Americas, New York, NY 10013–2473, USA

www.cambridge.org
Information on this title: www.cambridge.org/9780521787437

The *Cambridge Latin Course* is an outcome of work jointly commissioned by
the Schools Council before its closure and the Cambridge School Classics Project,
and is published under the aegis of the University of Cambridge School Classics
Project and the North American Cambridge Classics Project.

First published 1970
Second edition 1982
Third edition 1989
Fourth edition 2002
12th printing 2011

Printed in the United States of America

A catalog record for this publication is available from the British Library.

ISBN 978-0-521-78743-7 Workbook

Cambridge University Press has no responsibility for the persistence or
accuracy of URLs for external or third-party Internet Web sites referred to in
this publication and does not guarantee that any content on such Web sites is,
or will remain, accurate or appropriate. Information regarding prices, travel
timetables, and other factual information given in this work are correct at
the time of first printing. Cambridge University Press does not guarantee
the accuracy of such information thereafter.

Layout by Newton Harris Design Partnership
Illustrations: Joy Mellor, Leslie Jones, Peter Kesteven, and Neil Sutton; Fickle Fortune
by Jill Dalladay, Exitium II by Patricia Bell

Preface

This workbook is designed to be used in conjunction with Unit 3 of the **Cambridge Latin Course**. A variety of exercises is provided for each Stage:

- exercises consolidating Latin vocabulary and grammar;
- language awareness exercises, mainly involving work on Latin derivations in English and other modern languages;
- exercises testing oral and/or aural comprehension;
- exercises extending and testing knowledge of Classical mythology and the socio-historical settings of Unit 3;
- focused questions on each cultural section.

The *Key to the Omnibus Workbook* can be found in the Unit 3 *Teacher's Manual* (North American Fourth Edition).

This *Omnibus Workbook* is a selection of worksheets from the North American **Cambridge Latin Course** Unit 3 *Workbook* (editors Ed Phinney and Patricia Bell), from the NACCP *Unit 3 Treasure Box*, as well as new material created for the Fourth Edition by the Revision Team.

We would like to acknowledge the generosity of the many teachers who willingly shared their ideas and worksheets with us.

Lastly we should like to express our indebtedness to Fiona Kelly, our editor, for her expertise, patience, and hard work.

Patricia Bell
Stan Farrow
Stephanie Pope
Richard Popeck
Anne Shaw

Perfect your participles

Listen to the description for each of these pictures, and circle the correct missing participle.

1

a) honōrāta b) honōrātī c) honōrātus

2

a) parātae b) parātum c) parāta

3

a) excitātus b) excitātō c) excitātam

4

a) invītātī b) invītātō c) invītātus

5
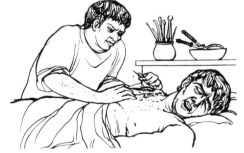
a) arcessīta b) arcessītus c) arcessītī

6

a) incitāta b) incitātī c) incitātus

7

a) laudātī b) laudātus c) laudāta

8

a) aedificātus b) aedificātum c) aedificātī

Lazy Memor

After you have studied the story
Lūcius Marcius Memor I, *answer the*
following questions by circling the
appropriate word in each column.
Then translate the sentence.

1 **Who was Lūcius Marcius Memor?**
   Lūcius Marcius Memor erat   faber   Rōmānus
                                haruspex   Britannicus
                                architectus   Graecus
                                servus   Aegyptius

2 **What kind of man was Lūcius Marcius Memor?**
   Lūcius Marcius Memor erat homō   parvus   et   sapiēns
                                     bonus   obēsus
                                     sordidus   pulcher
                                     ignāvus   decōrus

3 **Whom didn't Memor give a hoot about?**
   fortēs   floccī nōn faciēbat Memor.
   nōbilēs
   līberālēs
   aegrōtōs

4 **Whom did Memor consider of still less value?**
   Aegyptiōs   etiam minōris pretiī habēbat Memor.
   Syriōs
   Britannōs
   Rōmānōs

5 **What kind of soldiers were among the invalids?**
   mīlitēs ab hostibus   parātī   inter aegrōtōs erant.
                          arcessītī
                          vulnerātī
                          summersī

6 **What were the craftsmen doing when Cephalus sent them away?**
   fabrōs Memorem absentem   laudantēs   Cephalus dīmīsit.
                              interficientēs
                              vituperantēs
                              pulsantēs
                              verberantēs

6

21.3 Hear, Dare in Everywhere

Select the correct meaning for each of the following verb forms in boldface.

1 Cephalus Memorem **audit**.
   a) hears   b) dares   c) approaches   d) helps   e) is here

2 Clēmēns cum operīs pugnāre **audet**.
   a) hears   b) dares   c) approaches   d) helps   e) is near

3 astrologus dominō appropinquāre **audēbat**.
   a) used to hear   c) used to help
   b) used to dare   d) used to approach

4 Cogidubnus et Quīntus balneum **adeunt**.
   a) hear   b) dare   c) approach   d) help   e) are present

5 astrologus Barbillum **adiit**.
   a) heard   b) dared   c) approached   d) helped

6 Cephalus senātōrem **audīvit**.
   a) heard   b) dared   c) approached   d) helped

7 cūr Phormiō Barbillum **adiūvit**?
   a) did hear   b) did dare   c) did approach   d) did help

8 astrologus, nihil **audiēns**, cubiculō dominī appropinquāvit.
   a) helping   b) daring   c) hearing   d) approaching

9 tabernārius, nihil **audēns**, Clēmentem operāsque spectāvit.
   a) helping   b) daring   c) hearing   d) approaching

10 operae, Eutychum **adiuvantēs**, lībertō appropinquāvērunt.
    a) helping   b) hearing   c) approaching   d) daring

11 medicī, verba astrologī **audientēs**, saeviēbant.
    a) helping   b) hearing   c) approaching   d) daring

12 prīncipēs, rēgem **adeuntēs**, dōna offerēbant.
    a) helping   b) hearing   c) approaching   d) daring

13 servī, dīcere **audentēs**, dominum laudāvērunt.
    a) helping   b) hearing   c) approaching   d) daring

14 Cephalus, rēgem **adiēns**, eum laudāre coepit.
    a) being near   c) hearing
    b) daring   d) approaching

15 Quīntus, rēgem **adiuvāns**, ursam interfēcit.
    a) helping   b) daring   c) hearing   d) approaching

Inscriptional Insights at Aquae Sulis

The real-life Lucius Marcius Memor was an **haruspex**, or diviner, who, when visiting the sanctuary at Bath, would have supervised the sacrificing of animals on Sulis' altar. (In antiquity, altars were located outside the temples.) After Memor had inspected the entrails of the slaughtered animals, he would have foretold the future. (See the bronze liver in your textbook, page 58.) The number of **haruspicēs** in their religious order, **ōrdō haruspicum**, was limited to 60. Since it was rare for members of this small religious order to be assigned secular duties in such a small and distant province as Britannia, it is unlikely that the real-life Memor was ever **prōcūrātor**, or manager, of the baths at Aquae Sulis.

The real-life Memor dedicated a statue as a gift to Sulis Minerva in her sanctuary at Aquae Sulis. The plan below marks the position where archaeologists found Memor's inscribed base in 1965.

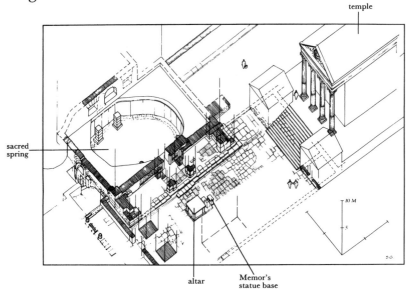

A 1 Study the picture of Memor's stone base in your textbook, page 12. Then fill in the missing letters below. Letters omitted from the inscription by abbreviation are set off in parentheses. The letter "V" was used as both the consonant "V" and the vowel "U".

> D _ _ _ S _ _ _
> L(VCIVS) M _ _ _ _ _ _ M _ _ _ _
> H _ _ V _ _ (EX)
> _ (ONO) _ (EDIT)

2 One common feature of Roman inscriptions is the "ligature" – the binding of two or more letters together as one. Find and copy two of the ligatures in the Memor inscription.

3 What is unusual about the positioning of the "O" in "MEMOR"?

4 What is unusual about the positioning of "VSP" in "HARVSP"? Suggest a reason why these letters, in a different carving hand, were added later.

5 Why do you think the inscription does not name the gift? In what grammatical case would the name of the gift have been written, if it had been inscribed there?

6 Translate the inscription.

B Here are two more inscriptions from Aquae Sulis, the first an altar inscription, the second a tombstone.

1 Both inscriptions display another common feature of Roman inscriptions, the "superlinear" letter. Write down the letter that is often carved as an upper extension of another letter.

2 Decipher each inscription, using the key for abbreviations provided below.

Roman Altar	English Translation
DEAE	
SVLIM	_ _ (the) _ _ _ _ _ _ _
N:RVAE	_ _ _ _ _ _ _ _ _ _ _ _ (lines 2–3 of the inscription)
SVLN̦S	_ _ _ _ _ _ _ ,
MATV	_ _ _ _ _ _ _ _ _ _ _ , (lines 5–6 of the inscription)
RI FIL	willingly and deservedly fulfilled his vow.
V·S·L·M	

Roman Tombstone	English Translation
D M	To the spirits of the departed
C(AIVS) CALPVRNIVS	Caius _ _ _ _ _ _ _ _ _ _
RECEPTVS SAC^{ER}	_ _ _ _ _ _ _ _
DOS DEAE SV	_ _ _ _ _ _ _ _ (the) _ _ _ _ _ _ _ _ _ _ _ _ (lines 3–5)
L S VIX AN LXXV	_ _ _ _ _ _ _ _ _ _ -_ _ _ _ _ _ _ _
CALPVRNA TRIFO	_ _ _ _ _ _ _ _ _ _ _ _ _ _
SA LBERT CON'VNX	(his) _ _ _ _ _ _ _ _ _ (and) _ _ _ _
F C	had this stone put up.

Latin Inscriptional Abbreviations

FIL = filius
VSLM
V = votum (vow, promise)
S = solvit (fulfilled)
L = libens (willingly)
M = merito (deservedly)

DM = dis manibus (to the
              spirits of the departed)
VIX = vixit
AN = annos
FC = faciendum curavit
     (had this stone set up)

Word Patterns

A *Study the forms and meanings of the following words:*

The suffix **-(i)ānus** and the suffix **-īnus** when added to a Latin noun form an adjective which means *of* or *pertaining to*.

canis	dog	**canīnus**	pertaining to a dog
leō	lion	**leōnīnus**	pertaining to a lion
mōns	mountain	**montānus**	pertaining to a mountain
silva	forest	**silvānus**	pertaining to a forest

Give a Latin adjective from the following nouns:

1 **ursa**   bear
2 **lupus** wolf
3 **fēlēs** cat
4 **mare**   sea
5 **mūs**   mouse

Suggest a meaning for the following adjectives:

6 **fēminīnus**
7 **cervīnus**
8 **urbānus**
9 **medicīnus**
10 **lībertīnus**
11 **Rōmānus**

B *Explain the following phrases or terms:*

1 an aquiline nose
2 canine teeth
3 serpentine walls
4 belonging to the murine family
5 an urbane individual
6 a leonine countenance
7 an asinine remark
8 a marine creature
9 a meadow of columbines
10 a notorious libertine
11 a sylvan scene

C *Explain the motto of West Virginia –* **montānī semper līberī**

10

21.6   Aquae Sulis and its Baths

Read pages 18–24 in your textbook and answer the following:

1. Where is Aquae Sulis? What is special about this place?

2. How much liquid is produced every day? What is its temperature? What is its composition?

3. What was the attitude of the pre-Roman Celts to this spring?

4. Who was Sulis and what was her power?

5. What did the Romans recognize about the area? What change in the area did they make?

6. What was the most important part of the bath complex?

7. Describe what the Romans built in this area.

8. What was thrown into the spring?

9. Why was the main building impressive?

10. Describe the types of baths and the water temperature of each.

11. Name two types of workmen who made this complex a wonder of Roman Britain.

12. Give two reasons why people were attracted to Aquae Sulis.

13. Describe the details of two tombstones found at Aquae Sulis.

14. What was the reason for building a temple dedicated to Sulis Minerva?

15. Describe the temple to Sulis Minerva and its precinct. Describe the statue which may have been inside the temple. Describe the pediment of the temple.

16. Why did the Romans link their goddess Minerva with the Celtic goddess, Sulis?

17. What was on the statue base found in the temple precinct? What does this suggest about the reputation of Aquae Sulis?

18. Suggest some of the other buildings that might have existed in the town.

19. What souvenirs might tourists have purchased there?

Character Traits

A *Your teacher will read aloud a description of each of the following characters. Write in the blank the letter of the correct description for each character.*

1 Cogidubnus est _____

2 Latrō est _____

3 Vilbia est _____

4 Salvius est _____

5 Bulbus est _____

6 Modestus est _____

7 Quīntus est _____

8 Imperātor Rōmānus est _____

9 Cephalus est _____

10 Memor est _____

B *The following superlatives would be an alternative way of describing some of the characters above. Supply a name for each adjective.*

1 callidissimus _____   4 optimus   _____

2 stultissima   _____   5 dīligentissimus _____

3 ignāvissimus _____   6 potentissimus   _____

Who said what?

Listen to the sentences your teacher will read and identify the likely speaker.

1 (Rubria, Vilbia, Bulbus)

2 (Modestus, Latro, Strythio)

3 (Rubria, Vilbia, Modestus)

4 (Strythio, Bulbus, Gutta)

5 (Cephalus, Memor, Cogidubnus)

6 (Strythio, Bulbus, Modestus)

22.3 **Finding the Common Denominator**

Read the following Latin clues and determine the person or place being described.

1 pecūniam dēbet
   puellam āmīsit
   ā mīlite ferōciter pulsātus
   humī iacēns
   puellam adeptus exit

2 fībulam ostendēns
   dēcepta ā mīlite Rōmānō
   lacertōs cōnspicāta statim eum amāvī
   thermās ingressa
   longē errāvī

3 haruspex
   sacerdōtēs
   templum ā fabrīs aedificātum
   dea ā multīs honōrāta
   fōns sacer

4 ā dominō vituperātus
   pōculum ā latrōne Aegyptiō datum
   rīsum cēlāns
   pōculum rēgī praebēns
   abīre iussus

13

dēfīxiōnēs

A *Who stole the bracelet?*

This **dēfīxiō** was inscribed on a square of sheet lead, cut into the shape of a cross.

NOMEN REI
QUI DESTRA-
LE INVOLAVE-
RIT

1   In the **dēfīxiō** above, what is the peculiarity of the "E"s? Of the "L"s?
2   With the help of the words below, translate the **dēfīxiō**.
3   By throwing this **dēfīxiō** into the spring of Sulis, the petitioner hoped to find out the name of the culprit. How do you think the goddess was supposed to reveal it?

B *What did Tretia Maria do?*

1   With the help of the words below, translate the following dēfīxiō:

TRETIAM MARIAM DEFICO ET ILLEUS VITAM MENTEM
ET MEMORIAM ET IOCINERA ET PULMONES INTERMIXTA

2   To complete the following statements correctly, check two items from the parentheses. Put the underlined letters of your two choices in the boxes.

a)   **dēfīxiōnēs** were made of (ir<u>o</u>n, <u>l</u>ead, pap<u>y</u>rus, <u>p</u>ewter).   ☐ ☐
b)   They are often found in (Roman bath<u>s</u>, a hyp<u>o</u>caust, w<u>e</u>lls, <u>b</u>asilicas).   ☐ ☐
c)   They were used to ask help from the gods of (thi<u>e</u>ves, the <u>U</u>nderworld, <u>A</u>quae Sulis, dea<u>t</u>h).   ☐ ☐
d)   To make messages mysterious, they were written (back to <u>f</u>ront, in black in<u>k</u>, <u>w</u>ith a long nail, with mean<u>i</u>ngless words).   ☐ ☐

3   Unscramble the eight letters above and find the word to complete this sentence.

Messages on **dēfīxiōnēs** were often _ _ _ _ _ _ _ _ .

reī: reus	*culprit*	illeus (= īllius)	*of her*
destrāle (= dextrāle)	*bracelet*	iocinera	*liver*
involāverit: involāre	*steal*	pulmōnēs	*lungs*
dēficō	*I curse*		

22.5 Question, Direction, Reflection

Your teacher will read you a series of questions. Circle the correct answer.

1 fūr sē (ante columnam/post columnam) cēlāvit.

2 senex (ā fonte/ad fontem) prōcessit.

3 senex amulētum (in fonte/in fontem) dēiēcit.

4 fūr amulētum (in aquā/in aquam) quaesīvit.

5 Bulbus saepe (dē mātrimōniō/sine mātrimōniō) locūtus nihil effēcit.

6 Strȳthiō fortūnātus (longē ā Modestō/prope Modestum) stetit.

7 amīcī (ad tabernam Latrōnis/ē tabernā Latrōnis) ambulābant.

8 Vilbia (ad culīnam/ē culīnā) vēnit.

9 necesse erat Modestō (in thermās/in thermīs) exspectāre.

10 Modestus sē (ē fonte/in fonte) extrāxit.

22.6 Word Power

A The suffix **-ālis** or **-īlis** also forms a Latin adjective meaning *of* or *pertaining to*.

Study the following Latin nouns and adjectives.

gēns	gentīlis	vōx	vōcālis
senex	senīlis	rēx	regālis
cīvis	cīvīlis	nāvis	nāvālis
puer	puerīlis	sacerdōs	sacerdōtālis

B *Explain the following terms or expressions. Give the Latin noun and adjective from which the English adjective is derived.*

1 puerile behavior
2 hostile actions
3 marital bliss
4 a vocal concert
5 the principal teacher
6 servile demeanor
7 a juvenile delinquent

Snake Sentences

Circle the words that correctly translate the English sentence.

1 **The citizens offered wine cups to the men.**

cīvis	pōcula	hominī	obtulit
cīvēs	pōculum	hominibus	obtulērunt

2 **The architect cackling found fault with the workman's dirty tongue.**

architectus	cachinnantem	lingua	sordidam	fabrī	vituperāvistī
architectum	cachinnāns	linguam	sordida	fabrō	vituperāvit

3 **The workmen, praised by the architect, were very happy.**

fabrī,	ad architectum	laudātī,	laetissimī	erant
faber,	ab architectō	laudantēs,	laetī	erat

4 **The workman was sculpting the statue of the goddess.**

faber	statuam	deae	sculpēbat
fabrum	statuae	deī	sculpsit

5 **The old man, holding the amulet, proceeded to the fountain.**

senēs,	amulēta	tenēns,	ad fontem	prōcessit
senex,	amulētum	tenentēs,	ā fonte	prōcessērunt

6 **The thief approached the baths cautiously.**

fūr	thermās	cautē	appropinquat
fūrem	thermīs	cautissimē	appropinquāvit

7 **The thief, having entered the baths, hurried to the fountain.**

fūrēs,	thermās	ingressus,	ā fonte	festīnāvit
fūr,	ā thermīs	ingressī,	ad fontem	festīnāvērunt

8 **The thieves, terrified by the old man, fled from the baths.**

fūr,	senem	perterritus,	ad thermās	fūgit
fūrēs,	ā sene	perterritī,	ē thermīs	fūgērunt

16

Another Braggart Soldier

Here is a skit about a braggart soldier and his buddy. This braggart is named Pyrgopolynices ("Fortress-Quite-Victorious" in Greek), and his buddy, Artotrogus ("Bread-Eater" in Greek). The story is based on Act 1, Scene 1 of *Miles Gloriosus*, a Latin play written *c.* 204 B.C. by Titus Maccius Plautus.

A *Read the following aloud with a friend, alternating parts.*

> *via in oppidō Graecō. prope viam est domus, in quā habitat Pyrgopolynīcēs. intrat Pyrgopolynīcēs. intrat quoque Artotrōgus, sed Pyrgopolynīcēs eum nōn videt.*

PYRG:	(*exclāmāns*) heus! servī! arma mea polīte! (*intrant duo servī, quī gladium scūtumque dominī accipiunt.*) necesse est armīs meīs, sīcut sōlī ipsī, fulgēre. sed ubi est Artotrōgus? (*exeunt servī.*)	5
ART:	adsum, domine. ō domine, quī omnium hominum maximus, fortissimus, pulcherrimus es – maior quidem quam Mārs ipse – quō modō tibi servīre possum?	
PYRG:	dīc mihi, quid dē illō proeliō … ?	10
ART:	(*interrumpēns*) hercle! libenter tibi commemorō illud proelium in quō septem mīlia hostium ūnō diē occīdistī.	
PYRG:	septem mīlia?	
ART:	centum et quīnquāgintā in Ciliciā, centum in Scytholatōniā, trīgintā Sardōrum, sexāgintā Macedoniōrum … summa est septem mīlia! ō factum mīrābile!	15
PYRG:	(*pudenter, sed clam glōriāns*) nihil erat.	
ART:	(*susurrāns*) sānē nihil erat! homō est mendāx ac nimis superbus. rē vērā ignāvissimus est, sed mihi placet eum semper laudāre, quod hōc modō cēnam ab eō comparāre possum.	20
PYRG:	ōlim habuistī libellum, in quō facta mea scrīpsistī. nōnne habēs nunc hunc libellum?	
ART:	ita vērō! sed vacuus est. nihil in eō scrīpsī, quod omnia facta tua in memoriā habeō!	25

polīte: polīre	*polish*	Sardōrum: Sardī	*the Sardinians*
scūtum: scūtum	*shield*	Macedoniōrum:	
quidem	*indeed*	Macedoniī	*the Macedonians*
interrumpēns:		factum: factum	*deed, achievement*
interrumpere	*interrupt*	pudenter	*modestly*
Ciliciā: Cilicia	*Cilicia (a country in*	glōriāns	*bragging, boasting*
	southern Asia Minor)	rē vērā	*in fact, truly*
Scytholatōniā:		hōc modō	*in this way*
Scytholatōnia	*Scytholatonia*	vacuus	*empty*
	(a non-existent		
	country)		

PYRG: vir magnae memoriae es!

ART: quod vir multī cibī sum.

PYRG: hodiē necesse est tibi mēcum magnificē cēnāre. sed plūs dē mē
nārrā!

ART: dīc mihi, quid dē illīs puellīs quae dē tē heri interrogābant? *30*

PYRG: quae puellae? quid rogābant?

ART: molestissimae erant. rogāvit ūna, "estne Achillēs?" "minimē,"
respondī, "est frāter eius." tum altera puella, "scīlicet,"
susurrāvit, "frāter Achillis. tam pulcher, tam fortis est! quantī
lacertī! velim eum rūrsus vidēre." *35*

PYRG: num tālia dīxērunt? hercle! nimis pulcher sum. puellae semper
mē vexant. hem! estne hōra ubi commodum est nōbīs domum
redīre et cēnam cōnsūmere?

ART: ita vērō, domine!

PYRG: bene! post mē ambulā! *40*

exeunt.

Achillēs (*gen.* Achillis)	*Achilles (greatest of the Greek heroes at Troy)*
scīlicet	*obviously*
hem!	*well!*

B *Answer the questions below.*

1 What does Pyrgopolynices order his slaves to do? How does he
insist his weapons look?

2 While ordering his slaves around, what does Pyrgopolynices
suddenly want to know (line 6)?

3 How does Artotrogus address Pyrgopolynices? To whom does
Artotrogus compare him? Identify this god.

4 What subject does Pyrgopolynices bring up? How does
Artotrogus respond (line 11)?

5 How many enemies does Artotrogus say Pyrgopolynices killed?

6 What is the actual sum of **centum et quīnquāgintā** and **centum
and trīgintā** and **sexāgintā**? Do you think Artotrogus' arithmetic
is bad? Or doesn't he care? Explain.

7 Suggest why **nihil erat** (line 17) may be truer than Pyrgopolynices
realizes.

8 What does Artotrogus realize about Pyrgopolynices in lines
18–19? About himself?

9 Artotrogus says that he has what Pyrgopolynices is asking about,
but it is **vacuus**. What reason does Artotrogus give for its being
vacuus? Suggest the real reason.

10 What does Pyrgopolynices promise Artotrogus? What does
Pyrgopolynices want to hear first?

11 What new topic does Artotrogus bring up (line 3)?

18

12 According to Artotrogus, whom did a girl confuse Pyrgopolynices with? What did Artotrogus tell her?

13 What did the second girl think of Pyrgopolynices? What did she say she would like to do?

14 Does Pyrgopolynices believe Artotrogus? Why or why not?

15 Where do Pyrgopolynices and Artotrogus go at the end of the play? Why do you think Pyrgopolynices orders Artotrogus to walk behind him?

16 Write a brief character sketch of Pyrgopolynices and of Artotrogus.

17 Write a brief character sketch of Modestus and of Strythio.

18 Compare and contrast Pyrgopolynices with Modestus and Artotrogus with Strythio.

22.9 Magic, Curses, and Superstitions

Read pages 41–42 in your textbook and answer the following:

1 What are **dēfīxiōnēs**?

2 What were these commonly made of?

3 What was the reason for using **dēfīxiōnēs**? How many **dēfīxiōnēs** have been found in Britain alone?

4 Describe at least five steps in the method of putting a curse on someone.

5 How did one woman use a **dēfīxiō** after her ring was stolen?

6 Decode and interpret the Latin in the **dēfīxiō** which mentions Vilbia.

7 What were two of the methods used to increase the mystery and effect of the **dēfīxiōnēs**?

8 What represented death in the **dēfīxiō** depicted on page 42?

9 Who was Charon? What was the River Styx?

10 From the final **dēfīxiō** in your textbook, list at least three punishments the writer prayed for.

11 How did the Romans tend to see their gods?

12 What were **ōmina**?

13 List three signs that might indicate impending danger.

14 List three precautions that might help avoid misfortune.

Fickle Fortune

Use the following information and materials to make a board game, Fickle Fortune, *through which you may gain some experience of bargaining with the gods.*

- Your GOAL is to reach square 100, achieving wealth, health, and security.
- Make FOUR COUNTERS in the Roman racing colors: green, red, blue and white.
- Make a SET OF 32 CARDS from the masters below, consisting of 1 x Fortuna, 1 x bull, 2 x cow, 3 x goat, 3 x lamb, 3 x sheep, 6 x pig, 6 x grain, 7 x wine.

How to play

1   There are 4 players. Each player receives one counter and 5 cards. Put the rest of the cards face down in the middle.

2   Take it in turns, clockwise, to throw 2 DICE and advance up the board the appropriate number of squares. The first person to throw Venus (two sixes), starts.

3   When you arrive on a word-square, follow the instructions. If you hold the card representing the sacrifice or offering which you are required to make, you must give that card to the pile, placing it under the other cards.

4   The Fortuna card may be used, like a joker, to replace any other card.

5   If two players arrive at the same square, the player who was there first is displaced and must go back 5 squares unless (s)he can sacrifice a pig to Jupiter Stator, in which case both players remain in the same square until their next throw.

6   The game finishes when someone reaches GOAL, or when the cards run out. If the cards run out first, the winner is the person with the most wealth in hand.

FORTUNA	VACCA COW	AGNUS LAMB	PORCUS PIG	FAR GRAIN
				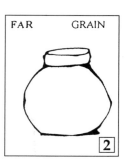
6	5	4	2	2

BOS BULL	CAPER GOAT	OVIS SHEEP	VINUM WINE

6	4	4	1

91	92	93	94	95 Your sacrificial goat ran away. Go back 7.	96	97 You run up debts with Salvius. Go back to START.	98	99	100 GOAL
90	89	88	87	86	85	84 Your wife is pregnant. Sacrifice a white pig to Juno or go back 2.	83	82	81
71	72 You start breeding peacocks for the table. Take a card and advance 9.	73	74	75	76	77	78 Profits are down and taxes are due. Sacrifice a pig to Ceres or go back 8.	79	80 You find a copper mine on your land. If you can offer wine to Vulcan, take two cards and advance 7.
70 Your farm steward dies. Offer the Lares wine and grain and ask for help or go back 11.	69	68	67	66	65 You have a new son. If you can offer a white lamb to Juno, take a card and advance 2.	64	63	62 You break your leg. Sacrifice a goat to Aesculapius or go back 6.	61
51	52	53	54 You make a good marriage. If you offer wine and grain to Juno, take a card and advance 1.	55 The rain rots your vines. Sacrifice a sheep to Bacchus or go back 9.	56	57	58	59	60
50 You find a sacred spring on your land. If you offer wine to the goddess of the spring, advance 11.	49	48	47 You have to make a long journey. Sacrifice a pig to Fortuna or go back 3.	46	45 If you can offer a bull to the gods to gain their favor, you may advance 12.	44	43 You buy a good slave to run your farm. If you can offer a pig to Ceres, take a card and advance 5.	42	41
31	32 Your harvest is nearly ripe, and the weather is bad. Offer a cow to Ceres or go back 4.	33	34	35 You recover from a long illness. If you sacrifice a pig to Ceres, advance 4.	36	37	38	39	40 Your haystack is burned down by lightning. Sacrifice grain to Jupiter or go back 10.
30	29	28 You win a bet on the racing. If you offer a goat to Fortuna, you may take a card and advance 3.	27	26	25	24 One of your slaves runs away. Make a grain offering to Mercury or go back 5.	23	22	21
11 Your aunt has left you her farm. If you offer wine to the Manes, you may take a card and advance 10.	12	13	14	15	16 You buy a job lot of slaves who turn out well. If you offer wine to the Lares, you may advance 6.	17	18	19	20
10	9 You have a new daughter. Sacrifice a lamb to Juno Lucasta or go back 1.	8	7	6 You retire from the army with a pension and a plot of land. Take a card and advance 8.	5	4	3	2	1 START

The Pediment of Sulis Minerva's Temple

Below is a drawing of the eastern pediment of the Temple of Sulis Minerva at Bath. Because the pediment now exists only in pieces, the artist has had to use logic and imagination to fill in some of the areas where pieces are missing.

Study the pediment, using the following guidelines. In the center of the pediment is a round shield, held high by two Victories depicted as two angel-like women. The Victories face the shield, and are standing on globes. At the apex of the pediment is the sun. In the corners are figures wearing drapery (like Hawaiian hula skirts), thought to be seaweed, and thus identifying the figures as sea deities, perhaps – as in the drawing – Tritons. They have long, coiling tails and are blowing conch shells. The helmet below the left Victory is shaped at the top somewhat like a snub-nosed dolphin; the helmet below the right Victory is topped by an owl.

In the center of the shield is a head which has been identified by some as a male Medusa, but by others as Sul (Old Irish for "eye" or "sun") with flame-like locks of hair, or even the giant Typhoeus, who personified geothermal activity.

After studying the myth of Athena/Minerva in handbooks of mythology, answer the following questions:

1 Which of the symbols in the pediment are linked with Minerva?

2 Which of the symbols in the pediment are linked with water?

3 Copy the picture of the head as given above and draw your own version of what you imagine might have been on the pediment. Keep to the triangular space in your design.

Word Power

A *Complete the following analogies:*

    1   misere : miserius : : paulum : ____

    2   celeriter : celerrime : : magnopere : ____

    3   facile : facilius : : male : ____

    4   facilius : difficilius : : magis : ____

    5   laetissime : miserrime : : pessime : ____

    6   simillime : dissimillime : : minime : ____

    7   pulchre : pulcherrime : : paulum : ____

    8   irate : iratius : : multum : ____

    9   benigne : durius : : paulum : ____

    10 ignave : fortiter : : male : ____

B *Complete the following formulae using comparatives from Stage 23:*

    1   A + better + ATE

    2   worse + ATIVE

    3   greater + TRATE

    4   AD + lesser + TRATE

C *Match the Latin word to its antonym.*

1	bene	a	minime
2	magnopere	b	pessime
3	magis	c	peius
4	maxime	d	paulum
5	melius	e	male
6	optime	f	minus

Minerva et Medūsa

When you have read this story, answer the questions that follow.

Medusa was the only mortal among the three Gorgon daughters of the sea-monster Phorcys. There are differing stories about how she came to look the way she did. This is a simplified version from the *Metamorphoses* by the Roman poet, Ovid (IV 794–803).

Medūsa ōlim erat puella clārissimae fōrmae, quam multī prīncipēs in mātrimōnium dūcere volēbant. in tōtā fōrmā nūlla pars fuit cōnspectior quam capillī.

  Neptūnus quondam, rēctor maris, illam puellam pulcherrimam in ipsō templō Minervae violāvit. dea āversāta oculōs tēxit. deinde, ubi Neptūnus ē templō ēgressus in mare suum dēscendit, Minerva, quod hoc scelus impūne esse nōluit, Gorgoneum crīnem turpēs mūtāvit in hydrōs.

  posteā Perseus herōs ā Minervā adiūtus Medūsam interfēcit caputque abscīdit. Minerva, dea potentissima et bellicōsa, quod attonitōs hostēs terrēre voluit, pectore in adversō anguēs, quōs fēcit, sustinuit.

fōrmae: fōrma	*beauty*
in mātrimōnium dūcere	*marry*
cōnspectior: cōnspectus	*striking, remarkable*
rēctor	*ruler, controller*
violāvit: violāre	*assault, rape*
āversāta: āversātus	*having turned away*
tēxit: tegere	*cover*
scelus: scelus	*wickedness*
impūne	*unpunished*
Gorgoneum: Gorgoneus	*Gorgon's*
turpēs: turpis	*ugly, unsightly (What noun does this adjective describe?)*
mūtāvit: mūtāre	*change, transform*
hydrōs: hydrus	*water snake*
Perseus	*Perseus (son of Jupiter and Danaë)*
herōs	*hero*
abscīdit: abscīdere	*cut off*
bellicōsa: bellicōsus	*warlike*
pectore in adversō	*in front of her breast*
anguēs: anguis	*snake*

1 What effect did the sight of Medusa have on viewers at the beginning of the story? at the end?
2 What ironies are there in Medusa's punishment?
3 Comment on Minerva's behavior throughout this story.

23.5 Dialogue Detection! Attempted Murder in the Baths!

A *Based on your reading of* **in thermīs**, *match the following people to the words they spoke.*

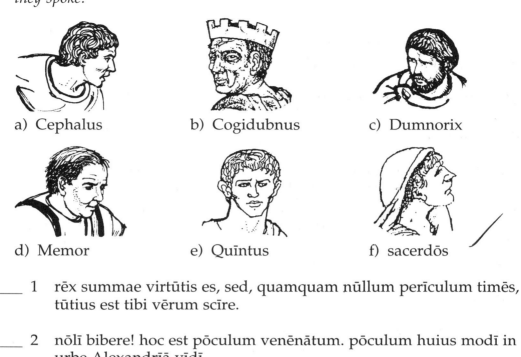

a) Cephalus   b) Cogidubnus   c) Dumnorix

d) Memor   e) Quīntus   f) sacerdōs

_____ 1 rēx summae virtūtis es, sed, quamquam nūllum perīculum timēs, tūtius est tibi vērum scīre.

_____ 2 nōlī bibere! hoc est pōculum venēnātum. pōculum huius modī in urbe Alexandrīā vīdī.

_____ 3 iubeō tē ōmina īnspicere. dīc mihi: quid vidēs?

_____ 4 pōculum īnspicere velim. da mihi!

_____ 5 facile est nōbīs vērum cognōscere. iubeō tē pōculum haurīre. num aquam bibere timēs?

_____ 6 iecur est lividum. nōnne hoc mortem significat? nōnne mortem virī clārī significat?

_____ 7 hae thermae maiōrēs sunt quam thermae Pompēiānae!

_____ 8 longē errās. nēmō mihi nocēre vult.

_____ 9 ōmina sunt optima! ōmina tibi remedium mīrābile significant, quod dea Sūlis Minerva tibi favet.

_____10 ubi est pōculum? nōbīs decōrum est aquam sacram bibere.

B *Which character above says nothing and is considered guilty?*

23.6 Roman Religious Beliefs

Read pages 57–62 in your textbook and answer the following:

1. Give three ways by which ancient people thought they could communicate their wishes to the gods.
   animal sacrifices, gifts, + prayers w/ promises

2. What type of gift would a general leaving for war offer?
   public ceremony w/ prayers + sacrifices (expensive)

3. List three reasons an ordinary person might offer sacrifices.
   successful business deal, safe voyage, or child birth

4. What type of sacrifice might be offered to Vesta and to the **larēs** and **penātēs**? What result was hoped for in return?
   food; to ensure the family's prosperity

5. List four other reasons people offered sacrifices and presents to the gods. honor them at festivals, thank them for success or escape for danger/some success, or to keep promise

6. What observations would an haruspex make in an attempt to interpret the **ōmina**? They would observe a sacrificed animals ever's size, shape, color, + texture to see if the omina were good/bad — is way small — vert!

7. How did **augurēs** attempt to discover the future?
   observing flight of birds

8. How did the Roman state react to the variety of gods, spirits, and rituals of its private citizens?
   Respected variety, but promoted worship of Jupiter + family

9. What did the Roman state particularly attempt to promote?
   worship of Jupiter + his family (Ceres, Juno, Minerva)

10. Who carried out the state rituals and ceremonies?
    colleges of priests/religious officials - senators (canous)

11. What religious position did Salvius have?
    Arval Brotherhood praying for brother + family (canous)

12. What was the emperor's role in religious practice? emperor family
    Pontifex Maximus/chief priest

13. Describe the correct rules of conduct during a religious ceremony.
    Stand still + silent, correct pronunciation, + pipe player to drown out

14. What was the attitude of the Romans to the religious beliefs of their subject peoples? Tolerant unless Romans own religious worship was threatened/worship no.1

15. What did the Romans encourage their subjects to do?
    Identify personal gods w/ Roman gods based on similar characteristic

16. What other feature of Roman religion encouraged acceptance of Roman rule in the provinces? worship of the emperor, eastern provinces had been encouraging worship of emperors

17. Describe how the emperor's **genius** was promoted in religion
    "Protecting spirit of emperor" linked w/ gods → worshipped Roman emperor

18. How was an emperor honored after death? Roman gods
    Deified through building temples

19. What happened to the Temple of Claudius in Camulodunum?
    Destroyed before finished by Queen Boudica's revolt in 60 AD

20. Which classes in the provinces supported the Romanization of religion? What were the positive effects of this policy?
    upper middle classes made Roman rule acceptable, reduced chance for uprisings + gave people sense of belonging

21. What method did astrologers use to predict the future?
    position/movement of stars/planets

22. What was an **hōrologos**?
    horoscope - position of stars at someone's birth

23. What was the official attitude towards astrology?
    Disapproving - if people used it to determine if relatives were going to die serious offense

Yes, No, Maybe?

Your teacher will read a series of questions to you. Circle the letter of the correct answer.

1 a) Salvius est homō melior quam Dumnorix.
    b) Salvius est homō peior quam Dumnorix.

2 a) ita vērō! Cogidubnus amīcōs suōs prōdere dēbet.
    b) minimē! Cogidubnus amīcōs suōs prōdere nōn dēbet.

3 a) ita vērō! Dumnorix Quīntō crēdere potest.
    b) minimē! Dumnorix Quīntō crēdere nōn potest.

4 a) est melius servō captō vērum dīcere.
    b) est peius servō captō vērum dīcere.

5 a) Modestus erat maior quam Strȳthiō.
    b) Modestus erat minor quam Strȳthiō.

6 a) ita vērō! fabrī ad aulam celerius quam aegrōtī redīre poterant.
    b) minimē! fabrī ad aulam lentius quam aegrōtī redīre poterant.

7 a) ita vērō! haruspex ignāvissimus aegrōtīs remedia praebēre vult.
    b) minimē! haruspex ignāvissimus aegrōtīs remedia nōn vult.

24.2 cum Quandaries

By selecting one item from each column form 8 Latin sentences. Do not use any item more than once. Translate each sentence into English.

Subjects	Cum Clauses	Completion of Main Clause
senātor prāvus	cum tabernam intrāvisset/intrāvissent	verba dīra dīcēbat/dīcēbant.
puellae callidae	cum flūmen trānsiisset/trānsiissent	coniūrātiōnem patefēcit/patefēcērunt.
mātrōna Rōmāna	cum pōns dēcidisset	flōrēs ēlēgit/ēlēgērunt.
iuvenēs perfidī	cum togam gereret/gererent	rēgem vīsitāvit/vīsitāvērunt.
haruspex trīstis	cum dē cīve perfidō cognōvissent/cognōvisset	equitēs monuērunt/monuit.
prīncipēs clārī	cum venēnum vīdissent/vīdisset	puellam cōnspexit/cōnspexērunt.
barbarī īnfestī	cum gemmās iniceret/inicerent	mandāta neglegēbat/neglegēbant.
mīles ignāvus	cum oppidum oppugnārent/oppugnāret	ōmina optima nūntiāvit/nūntiāvērunt.

fugitīvus

When you have read this story, answer the questions that follow.

Quīntus, cum equitēs Belimicī Dumnorigem interfēcissent, in silvās
effūgit. ibi multās hōrās manēbat. tandem, cum advesperāsceret, ad viam
rediit, quod ad Agricolam contendere voluit. tamen, cum flūminī
appropinquāret, duōs equitēs cōnspexit, pontem īnspicientēs.

Quīntus, graviter vulnerātus, trāns flūmen natāre nōluit, equitēs   5
superāre nōn potuit. itaque ad silvās regressus, dē vītā suā dēspērābat.

subitō ūnus equitum, "pondus grave," inquit, "hunc pontem dēlēvit."

"nēmō eum trānsīre potest," respondit alter.

haec verba locūtī, in equōs conscendērunt et discessērunt.

Quīntus, cum equitēs abiissent, pontem trānsīre temptāvit. tignum,   10
quod prope flūmen invēnerat, super lacūnam posuit et hōc modō ad
alteram rīpam tūtus pervēnit. ibi, ob vulnera fessus, humī cecidit, paene
exanimātus.

subitō vōcēs audīvit. duo Britannī, quī in scaphā nāvigābant, pontī
appropinquābant. Quīntus, cum eōs vīdisset, auxilium petere cōnstituit,   15
quod longius ambulāre nōn poterat.

"amīcī," clāmāvit, "mē adiuvāte! cīvis Rōmānus sum, quī ad
Agricolam contendō. necesse est mihi festīnāre, quod rēx Cogidubnus
magnō in perīculō est. inimīcī Cogidubnī mē necāre volunt. Agricola
sōlus rēgem servāre potest. mē ad Agricolam dūcite!"   20

Britannī Quīntum cautē īnspexērunt. tum ūnus

"nōs pauperēs sumus," inquit, "et iter perīculōsum est. sī tū pecūniam
nōbīs ..."

"ego satis pecūniae nōn habeō," respondit Quīntus, "sed hunc ānulum
vōbīs dare possum." tum Britannīs ānulum Barbillī ostendit. "nunc vōs   25
mē ad Agricolam dūcere vultis?"

"ita vērō," inquit Britannus. "venī nōbīscum ad casam nostram.
necesse est tibi dormīre, quod fessus es. necesse est nōbīs crās ad
Agricolam prōcēdere."

Quīntus, quamquam Britannīs cōnfīdere nōluit, cōnsēnsit. in scapham   30
cōnscendit et cum eīs ad casam rediit. cubiculum ingressus, in lectō
recubuit, statim obdormīvit.

postrīdiē cum in lectō adhūc manēret, vōcēs Britannōrum extrā
cubiculum audīvit. illī dissentiēbant:

"ānulus meus est," inquit ūnus. "ego prīmus dē pecūniā rogāvī.   35
cōnsilium meum erat."

"sī ānulus tuus est," respondit alter, "tū cīvem Rōmānum necā! num
tū timēs?"

"sed tū potentior es quam ego. facilius est tibi eum necāre."

"et facilius est mihi tē quoque necāre. ānulus meus est ..."   40

Quīntus perterritus rem sēcum cōgitābat:

"hercle! montem Vesuvium effūgī. operās Aegyptiās effūgī. equitēs Salviī effūgī. nunc hī Britannī mē necāre volunt. nusquam in terrā tūtus esse possum? necesse est mihi iterum effugere."

haec verba locūtus, per fenestram dēscendit.

advesperāsceret: advesperāscere	*grow dark, become dark*
trāns	*across*
natāre	*swim*
pondus	*weight*
tignum: tignum	*beam*
super	*above, over*
lacūnam: lacūna	*gap, opening*
ob	*because of*
cōnstituit: cōnstituere	*decide*
pauperēs: pauper	*poor*
crās	*tomorrow*
adhūc	*still*
fenestram: fenestra	*window*

1 What did Quintus do after Dumnorix's death? For how long?

2 Traveling on the main roads would have been dangerous. Why did Quintus do so?

3 What were the two cavalrymen doing?

4 What was Quintus forced to do? Why? What was his mood?

5 To what conclusion did the cavalrymen come? What action did they therefore take?

6 **pondus grave hunc pontem dēlēvit**. Suggest a possible explanation for this.

7 How did Quintus cross the bridge? What effect did his efforts have on him?

8 Whose voices did Quintus hear? Why did he decide to ask them for help?

9 Suggest why he would have stressed Cogidubnus' name in his request for help. Give two other pieces of information he included. For each, suggest how the Britons might have reacted.

10 What did Quintus offer the men in return for their help?

11 In response, how did one Briton propose handling the situation (2 points)? Why did Quintus agree to this solution?

12 What were the main details of the argument Quintus overheard the next day? How did he feel about this? What action did he take?

24.4 Filling the Gaps

Fill in the squares of the puzzle below with the English words for the following:

two-letter words for **minimē, nōs, sī, ā, aut**
three-letter words for **nunc, quō modō, euge, enim**
four-letter words for **dūrus, minus, moneō, plēnus, plūs, saxum, tamquam, tūtus, umquam**
five-letter words for **dēcipiō, circum, parcō, peior**
six-letter words for **maior, lentē**
seven-letter word for **minor**

24.5 Progress Report

The following is a collection of progressions. Fill in each blank with a word which fits the progression logically. For example: **rēs**, ____, **reī, rem,** ____ *The progression is the declension of a fifth declension noun in the singular. The first answer is* **reī** *(genitive singular), the second is* **rē** *(ablative singular).*

1 sānus, ____, mortuus

2 parvus, minor, ____

3 fortiter, ____, fortissimē

4 fīlius, ____, avus

5 miserē, miserius, ____

6 vīcus, ____, urbs

7 ____, diēs, mēnsis, ____

8 ____, melius, optimē

9 stāre, ____, iacēre, ____, stāre

10 nūllī, ____, nōnnūllī, multī, ____

11 ea, ____, ____, eam, eā

12 audiēbant, audīverant, audīrent, ____

24.6 Odd One Out

Based on meaning, which word does NOT belong in each group? Explain your choice.

1 virtūs   auctōritās   adeptus   amor   vērum
2 flūmen   fōns   pōns   unda   aqua   mare
3 eques   virtūs   haruspex   custōs   agricola   sacerdōs
4 balneum   pōns   caelum   carcer   aedificium
5 appropinquāre   ēgressus   adīre   ingressus   venīre
6 humus   rīpa   mare   lītus   terra   fundus
7 mercātor   pretium   vēndere   emere   adiuvāre
8 hostis   inimīcus   comes   īnfestus   perfidus
9 dīrus   perfidus   prāvus   molestus   sapiēns
10 trīstis   laetus   īrātus   aureus   sollicitus
11 prūdentia   bracchia   genua   iecur   iugulum   femur
12 verba   colloquium   passus   sermō   locūtus

Travel and Communication

Read pages 77–82 in your textbook and answer the following:

1 What made it possible to travel and trade throughout the Roman empire?

2 How many miles (kilometers) of roads existed at the peak of the empire?

3 Name two methods Roman surveyors used to lay out the roads.

4 Describe the four layers Vitruvius specified for road-building.

5 What was an **agger**? What two purposes did it serve?

6 What is the proof that Roman roads were skillfully constructed?

7 What were the two original purposes for building roads? What additional effect did they have?

8 Define the following terms: **cursus pūblicus, diplōma, mūtātiōnēs, mānsiōnēs**.

9 How many miles could an official courier ride in one day?

10 How were private letters delivered?

11 What were **itinerāria** used for? Describe them.

12 Give three ways people traveled on the roads.

13 Where would wealthy people stay when traveling?

14 Where did the poorer travelers stay? Describe the conditions there.

15 Describe another method of travel. What, according to Horace, sometimes went wrong with that method?

16 What was a third and more popular method of travel? Give six of the drawbacks to that form of travel.

Direct and Indirect Questions

In each sentence:

- *underline the clause which makes up the indirect question,*
- *circle the correct verb,*
- *translate the entire sentence,*
- *write in the bubbles **in English** what the direct questions would have been.*

Direct Questions   **Indirect Questions**

1 neque centuriō neque mīles
   sciēbat ubi Britannī (manērent,
   mānserant).

2 hospitēs rēgī Cogidubnō dīcere
   nōn poterant quō modō
   saltātrīx (apparēbat,
   appāruisset).

3 architectus scīre voluit cūr
   faber statuam deae (sculpēbat,
   sculperet).

33

Direct Questions	Indirect Questions

4 centuriō et mīles intellēxērunt quid captīvī (fēcissent, fēcerant).

5 mīles explōrātōrem Britannicum rogāvit cūr post horreum (stāret/stābat).

6 mīles explōrātōrem comprehendit et iterum rogāvit cūr castra Rōmāna (intrāvit/intrāvisset).

Direct Questions	Indirect Questions

7 centuriō mīlitem rogāvit ubi explōrātōrem Britannicum (invēnerat/invēnisset).

8 centuriō, cum nōn cognōscere posset quō modō explōrātor in castra (irrūpisset/irrumpēbat), mīlitem iussit explōrātōrem ad carcerem dūcere et eum torquēre.

9 Modestus portam apertam cōnspicātus, in animō volvēbat quō hostis (abiit/abiisset).

35

Word Power

A *Give an English derivative ending in -ent to match the following definitions.*
Use the word in brackets as a clue.

1 unrevealed [latēre]
2 an unfortunate occurrence [accidere]
3 not permanent; passing quickly [trānsīre]
4 hardworking [dīligere]
5 compelling, convincing [cōgere]
6 competent, able, capable [efficere]
7 disagreeing, especially from a majority opinion [dissentīre]

B *Put an English derivative ending in -ate in the blanks of the following*
paragraph. The root words are listed below in order of their appearance.

potēns	haesitāre	mandātum	ōrnātus	captīvus	potēns
haesitāre	mandātum	explicāre	mandātum	precātus	
haesitāre	administrāre	mandātum	testis	nōmen	

The _____(1) did not _____(2) to send a

_____(3) to the magistrate. The magistrate, in _____(4)

raiments, tried to _____(5) the _____(6) with flattering

words because he wanted to _____(7) before implementing the

_____(8). Therefore, he asked him to _____(9) the

details of the _____(10). The reply was clear, "Do not

_____(11) or _____(12) to _____(13) my

_____(14). If you do, you will die _____(15) and I will

_____(16) another candidate as magistrate."

25.3 The Roman Legionary Soldier

A *Label the armor and equipment of the legionary using the Latin words from the pool below.*

> **gladius pīlum scūtum lōrīca segmentāta cingulum caligae**

B On which side does the **mīles** wear his sword? Why does he carry it on that side?

C The Roman soldier originally had a leather helmet or **galea**. By the time of our stories the helmet was made of metal and was sometimes called the **cassis**.

D Which standard weapon cannot be seen in this picture?

The Legionary Soldier

Read pages 97–102 in your textbook and answer the following:

1 Give two characteristics of a **mīles**. How long was his tour of duty?

2 Approximately how many men were in a legion? Give three capabilities of a legion, excluding fighting wars.

3 What two details about a possible recruit did the **inquīsītiō** have to confirm?

4 According to Vegetius, what were four of the desirable characteristics of a recruit?

5 List five types of physical training for the new recruit.

6 Describe the weapons training of the new recruit.

7 What did Vegetius advise as the best way to use a sword?

8 Define and give one detail about each of the following pieces of equipment: **gladius**, **pugiō**, **scūtum**.

9 What was a **pīlum**? How long was it? How was it constructed? Describe how its construction made it an effective weapon.

10 List and describe six items the legionary soldier wore at the time of our stories.

11 List at least six items the legionary soldier had to carry on route marches.

12 What did the legionary soldiers have to do at the end of each day's march?

13 What did the fully trained legionary soldier spend much of his time doing?

14 List at least eight peacetime duties that have been recorded in inscriptional evidence.

15 What was the rate of pay during the reign of Domitian? List four of the deductions from that pay.

16 How would a soldier's life change if he were promoted?

17 What two things might a soldier receive on being discharged?

18 What fighting skills did the various auxiliary troops have? What type of auxiliary troop was the most important? List three ways in which this auxiliary troop was used.

19 What was the reward for an auxiliary soldier on being discharged?

Purpose Clauses

In each sentence, underline the clause which correctly gives the purpose, and then translate the entire sentence. The correct answers are based on the stories of Unit 2, Stage 20.

1   servī in vīllam revēnērunt;
    Barbillum portābant ut (eum
    necārent/eum in lectum pōnerent).

2   servī per vīllam quaerēbant ut
    (arāneās invenīrent/Barbillum
    sōlum relinquerent).

3   astrologus in cubiculum irrūpit ut
    (Barbillum pulsāret/mūrem in
    umerum Barbillī pōneret).

4   Phormiō ad urbem contendit ut
    (medicum peteret/templum Īsidis
    vīsitāret).

When you have read this story, answer the questions which follow.

Sevērus, mīles legiōnis secundae, erat homō prāvī ingeniī. ad valētūdinārium quondam ambulāvit ut medicum quaereret. ubi valētūdināriō appropinquāvit, claudicāre coepit. valētūdinārium ingressus, magnum gemitum dedit. in valētūdināriō sedēbat mīles quī medicum exspectābat. iuvenis erat vigintī annōrum.   5

"ubi est iste medicus?" rogāvit Sevērus. "vulnerātus sum."

"nescio, sed eum exspectō," respondit alter. "velim medicum mē ex valētūdināriō dīmittere. cupiō ad amīcōs redīre."

"quam stultus es!" exclāmāvit Sevērus. "num vīs mortem obīre? ego autem sum vir summae prūdentiae. velim medicum mē in valētūdināriō   10
dētinēre. cum barbarīs pugnāre nōlō."

"quō modō vulnerātus es, ō vir summae prūdentiae?" rogāvit mīles.

"ego ipse rem effēcī," respondit Sevērus. "amīcus, cui quīnque dēnāriōs dedī, mē vulnerāvit."

subitō medicus, cuius nōmen erat Māchāonidēs, in valētūdinārium   15
irrūpit īrātus. Sevērum cōnspicātus exclāmāvit,

"num rūrsus vulnerātus es? num mūlus tē rūrsus calcāvit? num coquus tibi venēnum rūrsus dedit?"

"mī Māchāonidā, cūr tam inīquus es?" rogāvit Sevērus.

"bonam causam habeō!" inquit ille. "nam ad castra hodiē vēnit novus   20
centuriō quī īrācundus est. mē ad prīncipia arcessīvit, quod gravēdō eum afflīgēbat. sed remedium ā mē parātum eī nōn placuit. remedium gustātum respuit et ē prīncipiīs mē ēiēcit."

"quid est nōmen centuriōnis?" rogāvit Sevērus.

"Titus Flāvius Cicātrīcula," respondit alter.   25

"quid dīxistī?" exclāmāvit Sevērus. "Titus Flāvius Cicātrīcula? ego eum cognōvī, et ille mē. cum enim in Germāniā mīlitārem, vītam meam reddidit miserrimam. necesse est mihi eum vītāre. valē, Māchāonidā! mihi ad amīcōs redeundum est. melius est cum barbarīs pugnāre quam in hīs castrīs manēre."   30

"siste, Sevēre!" clāmāvit medicus. "aeger es! perīculōsum est aegrīs sē exercēre."

Sevērus tamen ē valētūdināriō iam fūgerat praeceps.

valētūdinārium:		īrācundus	*bad-tempered*
valētūdinārium	*hospital*	gravēdō	*a cold*
claudicāre	*limp*	respuit: respuere	*spit out*
dētinēre	*detain, keep*	Cicātrīcula	*Cicatricula (a*
mūlus	*mule*		*name punning on*
calcāvit: calcāre	*trample, step on*		*cicātrīx "scar")*
inīquus	*unfair*	siste!	*stop!*

40

1   What kind of man was Severus?
2   Why did he go to the hospital?
3   What did he do when he approached it? What did he do when he entered it?
4   Who was already in the hospital? What was he doing there?
5   How old was this young man?
6   What did the young man want the doctor to do for him? Why (lines 7–8)?
7   What did Severus want the doctor to do for him? Why?
8   How did Severus get his wound?
9   Why do you think the doctor, when he entered, insulted Severus (lines 17–18)?
10 What had happened earlier to make the doctor so grumpy?
11 Why was Severus afraid of T. Flavius Cicatricula?
12 Why didn't Severus stay to have the doctor treat his wound?
13 Translate the following two quotations from Severus. Explain the apparent contradiction.

cum barbarīs pugnāre nōlō (line 11).
melius est cum barbarīs pugnāre quam in hīs castrīs manēre (lines 29–30).

26.3 Beware lookalikes!

Translate the following sentences, being careful to distinguish between similar endings.

1   clāmor canum puerum magnopere terrēbat.
2   stolae mercātōris fēminīs nōn placent.
3   strepitus urbis fēminīs Graecīs semper placēbat.
4   servī canī cibum cotīdiē dabant.
5   servī dē vītā Barbillī dēspērābant.
6   mercātor vīnum caupōnum Pompēiānōrum vituperāvit.
7   salūs exercitūs maximī momentī est.
8   fēmina nōmina mercātōrum tālium scit.
9   custōs hōs captīvōs in carcere retinēre voluit.
10 legiō mediō in oppidō ferōciter pugnābat.

Who's who?

Your teacher will read six Latin sentences each describing one of the soldiers below. Put the sentence number with the correct person and then identify that person by his proper name (e.g. Agricola).

26.5

Word Power

Match the Latin word to its antonym.

1	bellum	a	benignus
2	facinus	b	proximus
3	falsus	c	probus
4	fidēs	d	pāx
5	saevus	e	perfidia
6	ultimus	f	beneficium

Chain of Command in the Roman Legion

A *From the pool below, fill each blank with the military title which best matches the description of the duties.*

> aquilifer   centuriō   cornicēn   lēgātus legiōnis   optiō
> praefectus castrōrum   prīmus pīlus   signifer   tesserārius
> tribūnī angusticlāviī   tribūnus lāticlāvius

_____ 1 Commander-in-chief of a legion.
_____ 2 Nobleman who was learning the art of generalship.
_____ 3 Staff officers at legionary headquarters.
_____ 4 Commander in charge of camp organization and training.
_____ 5 Highest-ranking centurion of a legion.
_____ 6 Wearer of a lion's skin and bearer of the silver eagle.
_____ 7 Officer immediately responsible for training and discipline. He wore a transverse crest and carried a **vītis**.
_____ 8 Second to officer described in 7 above.
_____ 9 Junior officer in charge of guard duty.
_____ 10 Blower of circular trumpet who transmitted commands from commander to centuriate standard-bearers.
_____ 11 Standard-bearer.

B *Match each number in the drawing below to the correct Latin title of rank for the officers shown.*

_____ a) signifer   _____ d) cornicēn
_____ b) aquilifer   _____ e) centuriō
_____ c) lēgātus Augustī prō praetōre   _____ f) lēgātus legiōnis

43

26.7 The Organization of the Legion

Read pages 116–119 in your textbook and answer the following:

1 How many cohorts were there in a legion? How many centuries were there in cohorts two to ten? How many men were there in a century?

2 Which was the most prestigious unit? Describe its makeup.

3 Who were the **prīmī ōrdinēs**?

4 What were the duties of the **optiō**, the **signifer**, and the **tesserārius**?

5 Who formed the backbone of the legion?

6 How many of these officers were there? What were their duties? What item symbolized their rank?

7 How do we know they were important to the army?

8 Who was the **prīmus pīlus**?

9 Who was the **praefectus castrōrum**?

10 Give at least two details about each of the following: the **lēgātus**, the **tribūnus lāticlāvius**, the **tribūnī angusticlāviī**.

11 What was the main difference between senior officers and the centurions? Because of this difference, what did the senior officers have to do?

26.8 Agricola, Governor of Britain

Read pages 119–120 in your textbook and answer the following:

1 Give at least four details about Agricola's early life.

2 When did Agricola first go to Britain? In what capacity?

3 What was so important about this tour of duty in Britain?

4 After continuing his political career in Rome, Agricola returned to Britain. What position did he have in the army this time?

5 What did he do well at Viroconium? What two honors did it earn him?

6 In what capacity did he return to Britain for the third time?

7 List four military and four non-military accomplishments of Agricola while in Britain.

8 Give at least three details of Agricola's life after his recall from Britain.

The Fortress at Deva

A *From the pool of words below label the drawing of the fortress at Deva. Then answer the questions that follow.*

> prīncipia   praetōrium   via praetōria   via prīncipālis
> via quīntāna   vallum   basilica   amphitheātrum

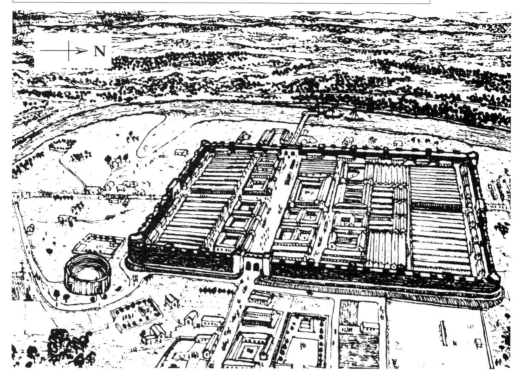

B What was the name of the wide street running west to east in this fortress? The modern street in Chester is still in the same position. The modern names are Watergate and Eastgate. Which end of it is now called Watergate?

C What was the name of the street running from the south to the **prīncipia**? The modern name of this street, which now runs across the entire city, is Bridge Street.

D What was the purpose of the **basilica**?

E What was the purpose of the room called the **sacellum**, on the north side of the basilica? Why was it **sacerrimum**, or the most holy place in the fortress? Why do you think the strong-room, with the pay and savings of the legionaries, was placed directly under the **sacellum**?

F Besides providing a site for entertainments such as gladiatorial games and beast fights, what more practical purposes did the amphitheater serve?

Direct and Indirect Commands

In each sentence:

- *underline the clause which makes up the indirect command,*
- *circle the correct verb,*
- *translate the entire sentence,*
- *write in the bubbles in English what the direct command would have been.*

Direct Commands   **Indirect Commands**

1   rēx Cogidubnus
    spectātōribus imperāvit ut
    saltātrīcī (plauserant,
    plauderent).

2   Quīntus Celerem ōrāvit ut
    alterum leōnem (pīnxerat,
    pingeret).

3   architectus fabrō persuādere
    temptābat ut labōrāre
    (dēsineret, dēsinēbat).

Direct Commands	**Indirect Commands**

4 Modestus Strȳthiōnem monēbat ut sub horreō sē (cēlābat, cēlāret).

5 Valerius mīlitibus imperābat ut fugitīvōs (quaererent, quaesīvērunt).

6 Vercobrix Britannīs persuādēbat ut impetum (fēcērunt, facerent).

Latin Logic

*Solve the following problems and answer the questions in boldface. In the first three problems, if you fill the boxes with **known** information, you can deduce the **unknown** information more easily.*

1 ōlim senex et iuvenis et puer templum vīsitāvērunt.
   cum senex iuvencum sacrificāvisset et aliī agnum et haedum
   sacrificāvissent,
   ūnus eōrum deīs gratiās ēgit,
   secundus saltāvit,
   tertius multōs versūs recitāvit.

   ille quī iuvencum sacrificāverat, saltāre nōn poterat.
   ille quī deīs grātiās ēgit, haedum sacrificāverat.
   iuvenis agnum nōn habēbat.
   quis deīs grātiās ēgit?
   quis saltāvit?
   quis multōs versūs recitāvit?

   iuvencum: iuvencus *young bull*

AGE	SACRIFICIAL ANIMAL	ACTION
senex		
iuvenis		
puer		

2 ōlim erant poēta et sculptor et pictor.
   ūnus eōrum erat aeger, secundus erat scurrīlis, tertius erat anxius.
   ūnus eōrum uxōrem suam offendit,
   secundus vīnum bibēbat,
   tertius iter fēcit.

   poēta erat scurrīlis.
   ille quī erat anxius, vīnum bibit.
   sculptor et ille quī erat aeger, uxōrēs nōn habēbant.
   quis iter fēcit?

PROFESSION	DESCRIPTION	ACTION
poēta		
sculptor		
pictor		

48

3 senātor et vīlicus et medicus in forō ambulābant.
ille quī togam praetextam gerēbat erat dīves.
lībertus quī forcipem sēcum portābat erat neglegēns.
vīlicus humilis erat miser.
quis erat nōbilis?
quis frūmentum portābat?

PROFESSION	ACTION	DESCRIPTION	SOCIAL STATUS
senātor			
medicus			
vīlicus			

27.4 Word Power

A *Match the Latin word to its antonym.*

1	anteā	a	vērus
2	ignārus	b	loquāx
3	praemium	c	posteā
4	silentium	d	raucus
5	falsus	e	sciēns
6	tacitus	f	poena
7	suāvis	g	strepitus

B *Copy the following words. Put parentheses around the Latin root from this Stage contained inside the derivatives; give the Latin word and its meaning from which the derivative comes.*

For example: conservation   con(serva)tion   servāre – to save

1	incendiary	6	tantamount
2	submarine	7	approximate
3	quality	8	tedious
4	jocular	9	noxious
5	osculate		

27.5 The Legionary Fortress

Read pages 134–138 in your textbook and answer the following:

1 If a legion was like a miniature army, to what could the legion's fortress be compared? Over how many acres (hectares) did it extend?

2 Define the following items and locate them on a plan of the fortress.
   a) **prīncipia**   e) **via praetōria**
   b) **praetōrium**   f) **via prīncipālis**
   c) **valētūdinārium**   g) **via quīntāna**
   d) **horrea**   h) **vallum**

3 List four defensive structures around the camp. What was on each side of the fortress? What was the heart of the fortress?

4 Describe the **basilica**.

5 What was the most sacred place in the fortress? What item was kept within it? Describe this item. What did it represent?

6 What constituted the worst possible disgrace and misfortune for a legion?

7 Who was an **aquilifer**?

8 What were the rooms on either side of the **sacellum** used for? What was close by or beneath the **sacellum**?

9 Describe the **praetōrium**. Who lived there? What three luxuries were found in the **praetōrium**? Why were they provided?

10 List three types of rooms in the **valētūdinārium**.

11 What were **horrea** designed to do? Describe four features of **horrea**.

12 What occupied the largest area of the fortress?

13 What was a **contubernium**?

14 Describe the set of rooms which provided accommodation for a **contubernium**.

15 How many men were housed in a block? Who lived at the ends of these blocks?

16 Give two reasons why the bath house was an important part of the fortress.

17 What structure was found outside the fortress? Give four uses of this structure.

18 What did civilians provide for military fortresses?

19 Describe the legal and actual practice regarding military–civilian marriage.

20 What were the **vīcī**?

21 What two roles did the fortresses play?

28.1   testāmentum Cogidubnī

A *Read page 145 in your textbook and summarize the details of Cogidubnus'*
will using the guidelines below.

I **hērēs** (lines 3–9)	1 Whom did Cogidubnus make his heir **ex honōre**? What reason did Cogidubnus give for naming this person? 2 What did Cogidubnus order his tribe to do? What reason did Cogidubnus give for making this request?			
II **dō, lēgō** (lines 10–22)	each person named in the will: 1 2 3 4 5	bequest or legacy item:	reason this person is given the item:	special instructions, if any:
III **mandō** (lines 23–28)	1 Who was named the executor of the will? 2 What instructions did Cogidubnus give to the executor of the will?			

B *Put a question mark beside each detail in the will which puzzles you.*

Salvius vēnālīcius

Translate the following story into English.

iam habēbat Salvius in Britanniā aulam, hortōs, lacum, vīllam. aula erat
ēlegāns, hortī lacūsque amoenī. vīlla tamen eī nōn placēbat, quod servī erant
molestī, lucrum minimum. Rūfillae quoque vīlla erat ōdiō. cōnstituit igitur
Salvius aulam, hortōs, lacum sibi et suīs retinēre, vīllamque vēndere. itaque
Salvius Euphranōrem, lībertum suum, quī ā ratiōnibus erat, arcessīvit.   5

Salvius: vīllam vēndere cōnstituī. illa mihi semper erat ōdiō. illam
                ēmī quod Rūfilla mē flāgitābat ut sibi darem. pecūniam,
                quam auctōre Rūfillā expendī, omnīnō perdidī. nunc tamen
                fortūnātus sum quod emptōrem invēnī. Gāius Iūlius
                Verānius, ūnus ex clientibus meīs, vīllam cupit.   10
Euphranor: quot dēnāriōs expendere vult?
Salvius: mīlle dēnāriōs.
Euphranor: quid dīcis, domine? audetne tantulum offerre? tibi
                cavendum est. Verānius rē vērā tē fraudāre vult. tē oportet
                pretium triplicāre.   15
Salvius: īnsānīs, Euphranor!
Euphranor: minimē, domine. sānā mente hoc dīcō. īnsānit tamen
                Verānius quod puellam pulcherrimam valdē amat. haec
                vīllam tuam cōnspicāta maximē cupit. Verānius amōre eius
                accēnsus recūsāre nōn audet.   20
Salvius: quō modō hoc cognōvistī?
Euphranor: amīcam habeō, quae Verāniō servit. spē praemiī rem mihi
                patefēcit.
Salvius: es homō callidissimus! quam prūdenter rēs meās cūrās!
Euphranor: dignitās tua mihi semper est cūrae.   25
Salvius: iubeō tē vīllam Verāniō vēndere. triplicā tamen pretium!
                eum nōn decet mē fraudāre.
Euphranor: sed, domine …
Salvius: quid vīs?
Euphranor: vēnde Verāniō vīllam sōlam! nōlī vēndere servōs quī in vīllā   30
                et agrīs labōrant. melius est eōs aliās vēndere.
Salvius: istōs servōs floccī nōn faciō. sunt hominēs sordidī et
                labōribus cōnfectī.
Euphranor: servī tibi sunt lucrō. nōbīs facile est eōs lavāre et exōrnāre.
Salvius: mī Euphranor, quis meōs servōs etiam lautōs emere velit?   35
Euphranor: domine, cōgitā! iam in aulā habitās; iam servōs rēgis bonaque
                rēgia accēpistī. facile igitur est tibi servōs tuōs vēndere quasi
                servī rēgis essent. hominēs semper ea quae rēgēs habuērunt
                emere cupiunt. tē oportet auctiōnem servōrum facere.
Salvius: quam perītē hanc rem cūrās! numquam lībertum habuī   40
                callidiōrem.

lacum: lacus	*lake*	tantulum	*so little*
amoenī: amoenus	*pleasant*	rē vērā	*in fact*
lucrum	*profit*	fraudāre	*cheat*
erat ōdiō	*was displeasing,*	triplicāre	*triple*
	hateful	accēnsus	*inflamed, burning*
ā ratiōnibus	*in charge of*	est cūrae	*is a matter of*
	accounts		*concern*
flāgitābat: flāgitāre	*nag at*	aliās	*at another time*
auctōre Rūfillā	*at Rufilla's*	labōribus	*worn out by*
	suggestion	cōnfectī	*hard work*
expendī: expendere	*spend*	sunt lucrō	*are an asset*
perdidī: perdere	*lose, waste*	lautōs: lautus	*washed, cleaned up*
emptōrem: emptor	*buyer*	quasi	*as if*

28.3 **Time Yourself**

*Cover half the page so that A sees only the A side and B sees only the B side.
A and B alternate reading the questions aloud. A reads the odd questions with B
selecting the correct answer. A verifies them. B then reads the even questions
with A selecting the correct answer, verified by B.*

A

1 quamdiū Modestus sub horreō cēlātus manēbat? (duōs diēs)

2 Salvius pecūniam (prīmō mēnse/ūnum mēnsem) extorquēre coepit.

3 quamdiū Belimicus Salvium adiuvābat? (trēs mēnsēs)

4 Quīntus iter ad Agricolam (sex diēs/sextō diē) faciēbat.

5 quandō Belimicus ad aulam vēnit? (nōnā hōrā)

6 Agricola ā Britanniā (septem annōs/septimō annō) discessit.

B

1 Modestus sub horreō cēlātus (duōs diēs/secundō diē) manēbat.

2 post mortem Cogidubnī, quandō Salvius pecūniam ā Britannīs extorquēre coepit? (prīmō mēnse)

3 Belimicus (tertiō mēnse/trēs mēnsēs) Salvium adiuvābat.

4 quamdiū Quīntus iter ad Agricolam faciēbat? (sex diēs)

5 Belimicus ad aulam (nōnā hōrā/novem hōrās) vēnit.

6 quandō discessit Agricola ā Britanniā? (septimō annō)

Word Power

A *Give an English derivative which fits each of the following definitions. Use the underlined word as a clue.*

1 A <u>proper</u> and fitting salary is a ____ wage.

2 One who was proven not to have <u>harmed</u> another is ____ .

3 A display which cost much money or <u>wealth</u> is ____ .

4 A person who works hard because he <u>is fond of</u> his work is ____ .

5 A guide in a museum who <u>teaches</u> visitors is called a ____ .

6 One who does <u>favors</u> for others can be described as ____ .

7 A person who has a large <u>body</u> can be called ____ .

B **testāmentum** is the name of the first story in Stage 28. **testāmentum** is composed of the noun **testis** – *witness* and the suffix **-mentum** which indicates the result of an action or the instrument/means of an action.

Following the same pattern, complete the chart below:

Latin Word	Meaning	Cognate Noun
complēre	to fill	complēmentum
impedīre		
ōrnāre		
sacer		
frangere		
īnstruere		
vestis		
docēre		
pingere		

28.5 Variations on an Ablative Theme

Make up 8–10 Latin sentences using some of the words listed below.
Use an ablative in each sentence. Include two sentences without nominatives.
Translate each sentence.

Nominative	Ablative	Participle	Accusative	Verb
hērēs	metū	incitātus	equitem	quaesīvī
hērēdēs	spē	incitātī	facinus	quaesīvit
comes	beneficiō	incitātum	armārium	quaesīvērunt
comitēs	corpōribus	vulnerātus	medicum	invēnī
centuriō	amphorīs	vulnerātī	iocum	invēnit
Modestus	clāmōribus	vulnerātum	triclīnium	invēnērunt
Rōmānī	pugiōne	complētus	ōsculum	vituperāvī
Britannī	perfidiā	complētī	ventrem	vituperāvit
explōrātor	venēnō	complētum	corpus	vituperāvērunt
fūr	cibō	dēlectātus	horreum	cupīvī
mīlitēs	īnsāniā	dēlectātī	coquum	cupīvit
mūrēs	ānulīs	dēlectātum	senātōrem	cupīvērunt

28.6 Roman Recipes

Sometime in the fourth century A.D., a collection of recipes, *De Re Coquinaria*, was made and ascribed to Apicius, the name of more than one Roman writer on food. The recipes range from Lucanian sausages, to asparagus, to chicken Parthian-style. Several recipes make use of garum.

Garum, also known as **liquāmen**, seems to have been a generic name for Roman fish-pickle. Garum was a combination of gills, intestines, and blood of a mackerel placed in a jar and covered with salt. To this mixture were added vinegar, parsley, wine and sweet herbs. The entire potion was left in the sun until the fish liquefied giving us the name **liquāmen**. After two or three months, a thick sauce resulted from this process and was used in various dishes. While there were other types of fish-pickle sauce, the one described here was fairly standard.

Consult your library or the Internet for an assortment of Roman recipes.

The Standard-Bearer

Below is a drawing of a tombstone from Deva of a **signifer** in the Roman army. The **signifer** carried the **signum**, or standard, of a cohort or century into battle. In peacetime, the **signifer** of a century kept the accounts of the men in his unit, deducting the amounts they owed for food and uniform, as well as a certain amount for savings. He wore a bear's skin with the head over his helmet, the pelt over his shoulders and back, and the forelegs tied at his neck.

A *Fill in the missing letters of the transcription of the inscription in the tombstone drawing. Letters omitted by abbreviation are in parentheses. Note that the singular genitive for **-ius** words is often **-ī** instead of **-iī**.*

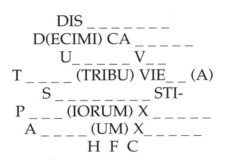

DIS _ _ _ _ _ _ _
D(ECIMI) CA _ _ _ _ _ _
U _ _ _ _ _ V _ _
T _ _ _ _ (TRIBU) VIE_ _ (A)
S _ _ _ _ _ _ _ _ STI-
P _ _ _ (IORUM) X _ _ _ _ _
A _ _ _ _ (UM) X_ _ _ _ _
H F C

B *Answer the following questions, re-reading pages 161–162 of your textbook if necessary.*

1 What was the soldier's name? What is unusual about the position of his cognomen?
2 What was his rank?
3 What was the name of his voting tribe?
4 Where was he born? (Hint: The modern name of the town is Vienne, in France.)
5 How long did he serve?
6 How long did he live?
7 What does **Dis Manibus** mean?
8 What does the abbreviation **H F C** mean?

Interpreting the Evidence

Read pages 156–162 in your textbook and answer the following:

Knowledge of the Roman occupation of Britain is based on three types of evidence:

I Literary Evidence

1 When did Julius Caesar come to Britain? Where did he land? How many times did he come? *55; landed @ southern coast of Britain, went 2 times to Britain*

2 About whom was Tacitus writing? What was this person's connection with Britain? How were Tacitus and this person related?

3 Explain the basis for bias in the writings of Julius Caesar and Tacitus.
Agricola, governor of Roman Britain, Tacitus's father-in-law
Caesar- justify actions to Roman senate/be favorable

II Archaeological Evidence
Taitus - wanted to honor father-in-law's memory/career

1 What is the task of the archaeologist? *uncover/explain past remains*
2 Give two of the ways sites are located. *accidentally; already known*
3 How was Fishbourne discovered? *workman was digging a drain in 1962- found fragments of mosaic floor*
4 What two things do archaeologists watch for on a site? What does this accomplish? *existence/position of any building foundations, way in which earth changes color + textures*
5 What else do archaeologists look for? Why? *small artifacts - bones, pottery, jewelry get as much knowledge about people who used buildings*
6 What two finds help in dating an excavation site? *coins/pottery patterns*
7 What information can pottery also reveal? *trade/travel patterns*
8 Trace the three-part development archaeologists have discovered on many sites in Britain. *simple timber farmhouse → larger stone house → grand, multi-roomed mansions*
9 What do excavations reveal about Roman activity in southeast Britain? about Roman activity in northwest Britain? *Peaceful/prosperous in SE /belligerent in the northwest Britain*
10 What is revealed by the excavation of roads? the excavation of Romano-British towns? the excavation of military sites? *communication, advancement of urban life*

III Inscriptional Evidence

1 What is the source for much of the inscriptional evidence about Roman Britain? *tombstones of dead soldiers*

2 Study the standard pattern for such inscriptions, given on page 161. Then examine the inscriptions on pages 162–163 and answer the questions that follow each.

urbs Rōma antīqua

What do you already know about ancient Rome?

Legendary Founding:	Geographical Location/Description:
Brief Political History:	Famous Roman Writers:
Famous Roman Buildings:	Famous Sayings about Rome:
Lasting Contributions of the Romans to Western Civilization:	

nox

This introduction is a good description of **Urbs Rōma** *by night. Read through the story on pages 169–170; notice the Latin adjectives and adverbs used to describe the feelings and atmosphere; answer the questions below:*

1   lines 1–3: It is a special night in A.D. 81. Describe what Rome is like this particular evening. Mention at least three items.

2   lines 4–7: In this story Rome is revealed as a city of contrasts. Write a translation for this paragraph which describes what the **dīvitēs** are accustomed to doing.

3   lines 8–11: Where do the **pauperēs** live? Describe what they are doing. Mention at least four items.

4   lines 12–21: From a general "panorama view" of Rome, the story shifts to a "close-up" of the **Via Sacra** in the **Forum Rōmānum** where the Arch of Titus is being completed. List six details of sound and/or sight found in this paragraph. Who is having the Arch of Titus built? How is this person related to Titus? What motive does he have for sponsoring this building project?

5   lines 22–28: What are Haterius and our good friend, Salvius, doing at the site of the Arch of Titus? List five Latin words which reveal their mood and feelings.

6   lines 29–33: Glitus, the foreman of the workmen, tries to soothe Haterius. Translate his words, lines 30–33.

7   lines 34–35: The Arch is finished. The City falls silent.

8   lines 36–39: Another section of the **Forum Rōmānum**. What is happening here? What are the two women singing/praying?

What's where in the center of Rome?

*Your teacher will read, in Latin, a description for each of the following monuments in and around the **Forum Rōmānum**. Write the number of the description on the correct line and add, in English, the name of the monument.*

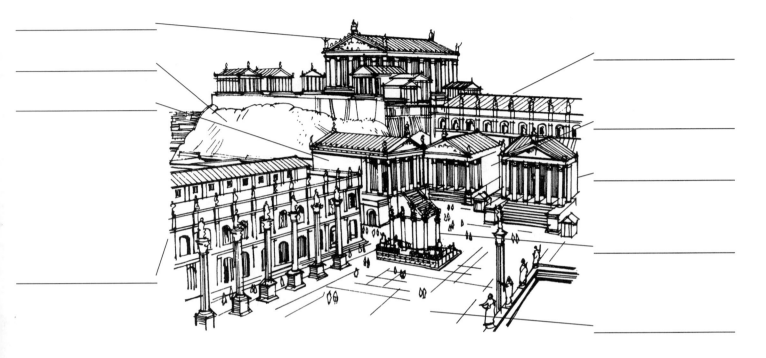

Personally Passive

Your teacher will read you a series of sentences. Circle the appropriate pronoun for the verb in each sentence.

1 ego, tū, nōs, vōs

2 ego, tū, nōs, vōs

3 ego, tū, nōs, vōs

4 ego, tū, nōs, vōs

5 ego, tū, nōs, vōs

6 ego, tū, nōs, vōs

7 ego, tū, nōs, vōs

8 ego, tū, nōs, vōs

9 ego, tū, nōs, vōs

10 ego, tū, nōs, vōs

11 ego, tū, nōs, vōs

Building the Arch of Titus

*After you have read the story **arcus Titī I**, page 177, answer the following questions by circling the appropriate word(s) in each column. Then translate each sentence.*

1 **quālis multitūdō ad arcum Titī conveniēbat?**

ingēns Iūdaeōrum multitūdō arcum Titī superābat ut īnsulam magnificam spectāret.
      Graecōrum   vīsitābat   lacrimam
      Rōmānōrum   sperābat   pompam

2 **quanta erat multitūdō?**

tanta erat multitūdō gladiātōrum ut multī populō appropinquāre nōn poterant.
                mercātōrum   arcuī persuādēre   possent.
                spectātōrum   fābulae crēdere   potuērunt.

3 **quālem locum invenīre volēbat Salvius?**

Salvius locum invenīre volēbat ubi Haterius Glitum   cōnspexit.
                              Rūfilla   amphitheātrum cōnspicit.
                              Quīntus   sē   cōnspiceret.
                              Imperātor Viam Sacram

4 **cūr in multitūdine aderat Haterius?**

Haterius aderat ut Titus   sibi   fāvit.
                  Imperātor Salviō favēbat.
                  Vitellia Titō favēret.

5 **cūr prope āram stābant haruspicēs?**

haruspicēs prope āram stābant

ut exta victimārum īnspiciēbant et fortūnam rēgnī   Rōmānī praedīxērunt.
               īnspexērunt   testāmentī   praedīcēbant.
               īnspicerent   imperiī   praedīcerent.

29.6   Word Power

A **virtūs** means *manliness* or *courage*. It is a compound of the noun **vir** and the suffix **-tūs**, referring to "the quality of."

For each of the following Latin nouns, give another Latin word to which it is related. Then give a meaning for the new word.

1   **iuventūs**
2   **senectūs**
3   **servitūs**

B   To what Latin verb is the noun **salūs** related? What is the connection in meaning?

29.7   Progressions

Fill in the blank with the word which properly completes the progression. These are based on Stages 25–29.

1   meus, _____ , suus

2   oppidum, _____ , imperium

3   _____ , puella, _____ , anus

4   _____ , morbus, mors

5   īnfantēs, _____ , iuvenēs, _____

6   noster, _____ , suus

7   _____ , centuriō, _____ , praefectus castrōrum

8   spēs, speī, _____ , spem, _____

9   contubernium, centuria, _____ , _____

10   rēpere, _____ , ruere, _____

11   _____ , rārē, _____ , saepe, semper

12   fīlia, _____ , avia

13   culter, pugiō, _____

29.8   The Origins of Rome

Read page 183 in your textbook and answer the following:

1 How did the Romans explain the name of their city? What is the traditional date for the founding of Rome?

2 What confirmation have archaeologists found for this tradition?

3 Who inhabited the surrounding area in the 8th century B.C.?

4 What were three advantages the city site had?

5 How did the site change from the 6th century onwards?

6 How many kings did Rome have? Who was the last king? What happened to him?

7 What changes in the government of Rome took place in 509 B.C.?

8 How did the government change again in the course of Augustus' life?

29.9   The Roman Forum

Read pages 185–186 in your textbook and answer the following:

1 Give four respects in which the Forum Romanum was the center of Rome.

2 What was the **mīliārium aureum**? Who set it up?

3 Name at least four other **fora** eventually built in this area of Rome. Which was the most splendid?

4 List at least five things a person could do in the Forum.

5 What was a **basilica**? What two activities went on there?

6 What was the **cūria**?

7 What two types of procession went through the Forum?

8 Where was the Forum located?

9 What was the main building on the Capitoline? Why was it so special? What two activities took place there?

10 Where did the Emperors live?

11 What was the **rostra**? Where was it located? From what did it get its name?

12 What famous event took place at the **rostra**? What was the result?

13 What were the distinguishing features of the Temple of Vesta? What was the important duty of the Vestal Virgins?

14 What was the Via Sacra? Where was it? What special events took place on it?

15 What monument was erected at the eastern end of the Via Sacra? Who commissioned it? What event did it commemorate?

16 What building was located between the **rostra** and the **cūria**? Who were held there?

29.10   Rome and Judea

Read page 187 in your textbook and answer the following:

1 When and after what event did Judea become a client state of Rome?

2 List three religious concessions that Caesar and Augustus made to the Jews.

3 By the time of our stories, what three aspects of life in Judea were causing unrest?

4 Who was the Emperor when this unrest escalated into a revolt against Roman rule?

5 Name the two Roman generals who were given the job of crushing the rebellion.

6 What happened to the first of these generals? What did the second general accomplish in Judea in A.D. 70?

7 Where and what was Masada?

8 Who went there and under whose leadership?

9 Name the legion and the general who eventually took Masada.

10 Name the historian who recorded these events.

Death of a Signifer

Below is a drawing of a tombstone from Viroconium (modern Wroxeter, England), the garrison of the XIVth Legion.

A *Study the inscription and then fill in the missing letters of the transcription. Letters omitted from the inscription by abbreviation are set off in parentheses. "V" is transcribed as the vowel "U" when appropriate.*

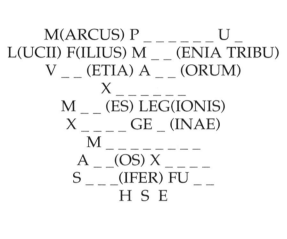

M(ARCUS) P _ _ _ _ _ _ U _
L(UCII) F(ILIUS) M _ _ (ENIA TRIBU)
V _ _ (ETIA) A _ _ (ORUM)
X _ _ _ _ _ _
M _ _ (ES) LEG(IONIS)
X _ _ _ _ GE _ (INAE)
M _ _ _ _ _ _ _ _
A _ _(OS) X _ _ _ _
S _ _ _(IFER) FU _ _
H S E

B *Answer the following questions:*

1 What was the soldier's name? (Note that no cognomen is given.)
2 What was his father's praenomen and nomen?
3 What was the name of his voting tribe?
4 Where was he born?
5 How long did he live?
6 What was the full name of the legion to which he belonged?
7 How long did he serve?
8 How old was he when he enlisted?
9 What was his rank in the legion?
10 What does the abbreviation **H S E** mean?

C *Translate the tombstone inscription.*

Particularly Passive

The difference between the active and passive voice is not so much a difference of meaning as a shift in the point of view.

A *Translate the following sentences:*

1 **active:** servī vīnum fundēbant.   **passive:** vīnum ā servīs fundēbātur.

2 **active:** puerī perītissimī   **passive:** versūs ā puerīs perītissimīs
   versūs recitābant.   recitābantur.

3 **active:** iuvenis mercātōrem furtī accūsābat.
   passive: mercātor ab iuvene furtī accūsābātur.

4 **active:** iūdex eum ad carcerem mīsit.
   passive: ab iūdice ad carcerem missus est.

5 **active:** pōcula iaciēbant; lectōs ēvertēbant; togās scindēbant.
   passive: pōcula ab eīs iaciēbantur; lectī (ab eīs) ēvertēbantur; togae
        (ab eīs) scindēbantur.

B *Circle the correct form of the verb in the parentheses, and then translate the sentence.*

1 clientēs dīligenter (labōrābant/labōrābantur) et semper patrōnum (adiuvābant/adiuvābantur).

2 sorōrēs ā patre Rōmam (mīsērunt/missae sunt) et ibi ā Vitelliā (acceptae sunt/accēpērunt).

66

Derivative Decision

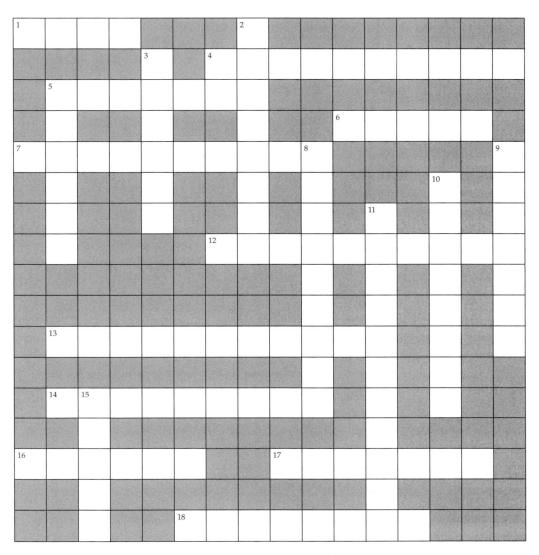

ACROSS

1 a work; a musical composition [opus]
4 the killing of one's sister [soror]
5 a light umbrella [sōl]
6 *Rigoletto, Tristan und Isolde*, or *La Bohème*, for example [opus]
7 dismal, gloomy, tomblike [sepulcrum]
12 having simultaneous conflicting feelings [ambō]
13 violent, turbulent [tempestās]
14 harmful, damaging [iniūria]
16 belonging to a locality by birth [nātus]
17 causing doubt [dubium]
18 a small or trivial work [opus]

DOWN

2 a sun room [sōl]
3 unnatural paleness [pallēscere]
4 the meaning of **tam**
5 fast (in music) [praestāre]
8 causing laughter [lūdus]
9 to decorate with a garland of flowers [fēstus]
10 a living being [creāre]
11 suitable for a master [magister]
15 connected with one's birth [nātus]

polyspaston

Write in the blank the letter of the correct completion based on the story on pages 197–198 of your textbook.

1 **Haterius Salvium ＿＿＿ dūxit ut polyspaston eī ostenderet.**
   a) ad forum   b) ad amphitheātrum   c) ad āream suam

2 **columnae ＿＿＿ secābantur.**
   a) ex saxō   b) ex marmore   c) ex lignō

3 **in tignō polyspastī erat ＿＿＿ .**
   a) sēdēs
   b) massa marmoris
   c) servus

4 **Haterius Salviō ＿＿＿ praestāre volēbat.**
   a) urbis magnitūdinem
   b) urbis prōspectum
   c) fabrōs

5 **Salvius, ubi sēdem in tignō fīxam vīdit, ＿＿＿ .**
   a) clāmāvit
   b) rīdēbat
   c) palluit

6 **fabrī ＿＿＿ tignum ad caelum tollēbant.**
   a) fūnibus
   b) oculīs clausīs
   c) rēbus magicīs

7 **Salvius, oculīs apertīs, ＿＿＿ vidēre poterat.**
   a) flūmen sōlum
   b) arcum sōlum
   c) tōtam urbem

8 **Salvius Hateriō ＿＿＿ offerēbat.**
   a) pecūniam
   b) agellum
   c) praemium

9 **Salvius prō agellō sestertium ＿＿＿ postulābat.**
   a) mīlle
   b) trīciēns
   c) vīciēns

10 **Haterius humum rediit, ＿＿＿ .**
   a) pecūniā contentus
   b) admīrātiōne affectus
   c) spē immortālitātis ēlātus

68

Word Power

Complete the following analogies with a word from the Vocabulary Checklist:

1 lūna : nox : : ____ : diēs
2 amīcus : hostis : : beneficium : ____
3 fēmina : vir : : ____ : frāter

4 ignāvus : fortis : : pauper : ____
5 īra : ērubēscere : : timor : ____
6 pauca : multī : : haudquāquam : ____

30.6 Audīte/Dīcite

Cover half the page so that A sees only the A side and B sees only the B side. A and B alternate reading the questions aloud. A reads the odd questions with B selecting the correct answer. A verifies them. B then reads the even questions with A selecting the correct answer, verified by B.

A

1 dīvitiās cupiō. quōcum mihi dīcendum est?
   (cum argentāriō tibi dīcendum est.)
2 sōl est in tabernā.
   sōl est in caelō.
3 quō nōs oportet mortuum pōnere?
   (vōs oportet mortuum in sepulcrum pōnere.)
4 hās iniūriās in bellō accēpī.
   hās iniūriās in salūte accēpī.
5 ubi sēdēs fīxa erat?
   (sēdēs in tignō fīxa erat.)
6 omnēs ad timōrem festīnant.
   omnēs ad lūdōs festīnant.
7 unde iuvenēs effugere volēbant?
   (iuvenēs ā strepitū Galatēae effugere volēbant.)

8 magister erat cum fabrīs.
   magister erat cum tempestātibus.
9 cūr līberī sē in cubiculō cēlāvērunt?
   (līberī pavōre cōnfectī sē in cubiculō cēlāvērunt.)

10 sine sorōre opus ante lūcem cōnficere possum.
    sine dubiō opus ante lūcem cōnficere possum.

B

1 cum poētā tibi dīcendum est.
   cum argentāriō tibi dīcendum est.

2 ubi est sōl?
   (sōl est in caelō.)
3 vōs oportet mortuum in sepulcrum pōnere.
   vōs oportet mortuum in argentāriā pōnere.
4 ubi illās iniūriās accēpistī?
   (hās iniūriās in bellō accēpī.)
5 sēdēs in tignō fīxa erat.
   sēdēs in templō fīxa erat.
6 quō festīnant omnēs?
   (omnēs ad lūdōs festīnant.)
7 iuvenēs ā pulchritūdine Helenae effugere volēbant.
   iuvenēs ā strepitū Galatēae effugere volēbant.
8 ubi erat magister?
   (magister erat cum fabrīs.)
9 līberī pavōre cōnfectī sē in cubiculō cēlāvērunt.
   līberī gaudiō affectī sē in cubiculō cēlāvērunt.
10 opusne ante lūcem cōnficere potes?
    (sine dubiō opus ante lūcem cōnficere possum.)

Roman Engineering

Read pages 203–207 in your textbook and answer the following:

1 How do we know anything about the Haterii family? Give two facts we can deduce from that evidence.
The crane, contract to Emperor Titus ← was a building contractor *one member of family*

2 What did an architect contribute to a building project?
Provided the designs, technical advice

3 What was the social status of the unskilled laborers?
slaves/poor freemen

4 List three of the jobs of the carpenters. List four of the jobs of the masons. *carpenter put up timber framework, gave shape + temp rary support to arches, rebuilt scaffolding, timber molds*

Masons
-quarrying/ transport of stone to building city
= cut stone to position
-preparing blocks to be lifted into position

5 List at least four hand tools that we have inherited almost unchanged from the Romans. Why was the use of hand tools so laborious in Roman times? *mallets, chisels, crowbars, trowels - didn't have electric motor*

6 What were the main ingredients in cement?
lime, mortar, fine sand, clay + water

7 What was cement mortar used for?
thin, adhesive layers blw stones

8 What were the ingredients of **opus caementicium**?
cement + rubble, broken bricks, pieces of tile

9 Name two main structural uses of concrete.
arches + vaulted ceilings

10 Name three structures in Rome which were built of concrete.
aqueducts/ Pantheon/ Colosseum

11 Describe another use of concrete and give at least four ways the concrete was hidden. *core blw 2 faces of expensive material, plaster, stucco, paint, marble*

12 Describe the **insulae** by noting the quality of construction, the building materials, and the danger inherent in such buildings.
made of brick, timber, could catch on fire

13 What two things did Augustus do to minimize the risk?
limit height to 70 ft, fires, organized fire lines

14 Who was Emperor during the Great Fire of A.D. 64? Why, according to to Tacitus, did the fire spread so fast?
Nero was emperor, travelled quickly on hills long alle

15 Name at least five buildings either restored by Domitian after the fire in A.D. 80 or erected as part of his building program.
temple of Jupiter, Flavian Amp, Titus' Arch, Palatine Palace concert hall

16 What was Augustus' famous quotation on his work in Rome?
"I found Rome a city of brick, left it made of marble"

17 What contrast in use and construction materials was evident in the buildings of Rome? *construction of marble public areas next to ordinary residences*

18 Why was being a builder or contractor a lucrative profession during the reign of Domitian? *Domitian decreed it to add to city's splendor - kept builders busy*

31.1 A Ship from Greece

From the Latin sentences beneath the picture, select the one which is most appropriate for each box, write its number in the box, and then translate its Latin sentence in the box.

1 sōle ortō duo saccāriī sarcinās ē nāve expōnēbant.
2 haec nāvis ā Graeciā Rōmam advēnerat.
3 multī pauperēs Rōmānī magnīs in īnsulīs habitābant, quārum multae erant in Subūrā.
4 templum Aesculāpiī mediō in flūmine Tiberī stābat.

31.2 Result Clauses

Underline the correct form of the verb, and then translate the sentence.

1 clientēs tantam spem habēbant ut extrā iānuam (manēbant/manērent).

2 praecō tam superbus erat ut nihil prīmō (dīxit/dīceret).

3 tandem praecō tam paucōs dēnāriōs spargēbat ut clientēs eōs raperent et statim (cēlārent/cēlāvērunt).

4 adeō Euphrosynē taedēbat praecōnis ut discēdere (cuperet/cupiēbat).

Perceiving the Prepositions

A *Translate the following sentences:*

1 lēgātus in castra equitāvit.
2 optiō in castrīs ambulābat.
3 Belimicus pugiōnem in Salvium coniēcit.
4 Iūdaeī saxa in capita mīlitum Rōmānōrum iaciēbant.
5 mīlitēs in prīncipiīs conveniēbant.

B *Fill in each blank with the appropriate prepositional phrase. Then translate each sentence.*

> **in forō   per forum   sub Capitōliō**
> **prope forum   ab Imperātōre   apud populum**

1 arcus Titī _____ dedicātus est.

2 _____ est mōns nōtissimus, quī Capitōlium appellātur.

3 in forō contiōnēs _____ habēbantur.

4 _____ est templum Vestae.

5 aliquandō pompae splendidae _____ dūcuntur.

6 _____ iacet forum Rōmānum.

C *Change each noun in the parentheses to the correct case required by its preposition. Then translate each sentence.*

1 nunc Rōmānī nōs Iūdaeōs in _____ (servitūs, servitūtis, f.) trahere parant.

2 post _____ (tubicen, tubicinis, m.) vēnērunt iuvenēs.

3 taurī ā iuvenibus ad _____ (sacrificium, sacrificiī, n.) dūcēbantur.

4 Haterius, sine _____ (dubium, dubiī, n.), ut arcum splendidum cōnficeret, nimis labōrāvit.

5 Salvius in _____ (tignum, tignī, n.) sedēns ad caelum tollēbātur.

A Bird's-Eye View of Rome

Study the following map. Match the name of the building or area in Rome to its numbered location on the map by writing the number in the blank beside the name.

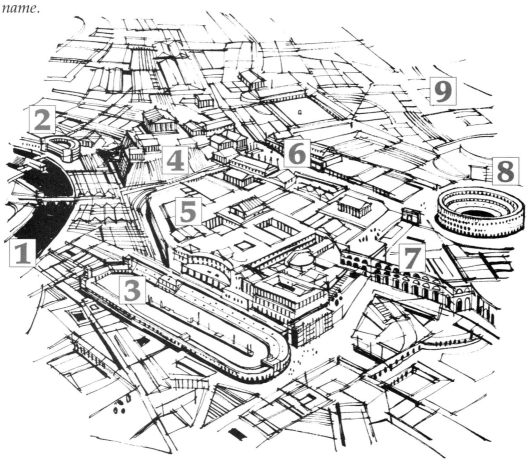

Rome as it was in the 4th century A.D.

_____ a) the Forum Romanum

_____ b) the Flavian Amphitheater

_____ c) the Capitoline Hill with the Temple of Jupiter Optimus Maximus

_____ d) the Theater of Marcellus

_____ e) an aqueduct

_____ f) the Circus Maximus, used for chariot racing

_____ g) the Subura

_____ h) the Tiber River

_____ i) the Palatine Hill with the emperor's palace on it

Command Performances

*This activity follows the format of previous Audīte/Dīcite exercises, but requires
two members per team. Cover half the page. Team A sees only the A side, and
Team B sees only the B side. Team A gives the odd-numbered commands and
Team B gives the even-numbered commands. The number (1) beside a command
indicates that one person gives the command. The number (2) beside a command
indicates that both team members give the command. If the command is singular,
only one person from the other team reports it in the "answer." If the command
is plural, both team members report it. The team giving the command verifies the
correct report as well as the correct number of team members reporting.*

A

1 (1) audī!
   (tū mihi imperāvistī ut audīrem. (1))

2 tū mihi imperāvistī nē dormīrem.
   vōs mihi imperāvistis nē dormīrem.

3 (2) tacēte!
   (vōs nōbīs imperāvistis ut
   tacērēmus. (2))

4 tū mihi imperāvistī ut pecūniam
   numerārem.
   vōs nōbīs imperāvistis ut pecūniam
   numerārēmus.

5 (2) surge!
   (vōs mihi imperāvistis ut surgerem. (1))

6 vōs nōbīs imperāvistis nē rīdērēmus.
   tū nōbīs imperāvistī nē rīdērēmus.

7 (1) cantāte!
   (tū nōbīs imperāvistī ut cantārēmus. (2))

8 vōs mihi imperāvistis ut abīrem.
   vōs nōbīs imperāvistis ut abīrēmus.

9 (1) nōlī labōrāre dēsinere!
   (tū mihi imperāvistī nē labōrāre
   dēsinerem. (1))

10 vōs mihi imperāvistis ut pictūram
   pingerem.
   tū mihi imperāvistī ut pictūram pingerem.

B

1 tū mihi imperāvistī ut audīrem.
   vōs nōbīs imperāvistis ut audīrēmus.

2 (1) nōlī dormīre!
   (tū mihi imperāvistī nē dormīrem. (1))

3 vōs mihi imperāvistis ut tacērem.
   vōs nōbīs imperāvistis ut tacērēmus.

4 (2) pecūniam numerāte!
   (vōs nōbīs imperāvistis ut pecūniam
   numerārēmus. (2))

5 vōs mihi imperāvistis ut surgerem.
   tū nōbīs imperāvistī ut surgerēmus.

6 (1) nōlīte rīdēre!
   (tū nōbīs imperāvistī nē rīdērēmus. (2))

7 tū nōbīs imperāvistī ut cantārēmus.
   tū mihi imperāvistī ut cantārem.

8 (2) abī!
   (vōs mihi imperāvistis ut abīrem. (1))

9 vōs nōbīs imperāvistis nē labōrāre
   dēsinerēmus.
   tū mihi imperāvistī nē labōrāre
   dēsinerem.

10 (1) pictūram pinge!
   (tū mihi imperāvistī ut pictūram
   pingerem. (1))

31.6 Antonyms

Match the Latin word to its antonym. Give the meanings of both words.

1	angustus	a)	frangere
2	ubique	b)	solvere
3	vincīre	c)	nusquam
4	ante	d)	post
5	reficere	e)	lātus
6	altus	f)	brevis

31.7 The "-ize" have it.

*The following **-ize** words are derived from Latin words which appear in the stories in Stage 31. Match the meaning to the English derivative.*

1	demoralize	a)	to proclaim in public
2	extemporize	b)	to impoverish
3	patronize	c)	to divide into geographical areas
4	pauperize	d)	to exercise the voice
5	philosophize	e)	to frequent as a customer
6	preconize	f)	to gain the attention of the public
7	publicize	g)	to theorize
8	sectionalize	h)	to speak without preparation; to improvise
9	visualize	i)	to form a mental image
10	vocalize	j)	to weaken the spirit of; to throw into confusion

31.8 The City of Rome

Read pages 224–228 in your textbook and answer the following:

1 Describe the city of Rome in terms of design and population density.
  unplanned / unsystematic - crowded apartsments w/ commercial building
2 What was Ostia?
  Rome's coastal port @ T-River mouth
3 Give two pieces of information about Ostia.
  began under Claudius - large warehouses
4 What river connects Ostia with Rome? How do we know it was navigable up to the City? T. River; had riverside markets (emporia) + warehouses (horrea)

75

5 Describe the **īnsula Tiberīna**. *ornamental prow - rostrum*
elongated island that had a temple for Asclepius
6 Outline the route Euphrosyne and her slave would have taken to
reach Haterius' house *around lower Capitoline hill + through*
the roman forum + past the Palatine hill
7 Describe the **Subura**: its appearance and its inhabitants.
densely populated district normal turn, large tenement houses
8 In what way did the **Subura** differ from the Esquiline area?
Subura was a densely populated area w/ tenement buildings [insula] - poor people
9 Identify two places of entertainment in central Rome.
Circus maximus (chariot races) + colosseum
Esquiline rich, stately mansions w/ wealthy
10 Where was the **Campus Martius**? How had it once been used? What
did it provide in Domitian's time? *Was an army training area -*
provided open space in his time
11 What was the purpose of the aqueducts? What was their daily
capacity? *bring H₂O into city, 200 m gallons / day.*

12 Compare how the rich and poor obtained their water.
Rich had direct pipelines to water, poor had public fountains
13 What was the **Cloaca Maxima**? How did it function?
central drain carrying sewage to water into Tiber
14 What were some of the disadvantages for people living in Rome?
congestion, overcrowding, frequent fires, unhealed
trash were burned

31.9 Patronage and Roman Society

Read pages 229–232 in your textbook and answer the following:

1 What did clients hope for from a patron? What did a patron expect
from clients in return? *clients gave services, while patrons*
gave protection + food
2 What does **salūtātiō** mean? *morning call*
3 What kinds of people were involved in the procedure of **salūtātiō**?
patrons / clients rich people / poor people (except for emperor)
4 How had patronage changed by the time of our stories?
people who really need / had money
5 What role did the **toga** and **sportula** play in the system described?
toga - what they wore, sportula - baskets for food
6 What humiliation might a client have undergone when invited to
dinner? *being served food were inferior to that of the guests*
7 What two writers often mention the system of patronage? Why
should we be careful in accepting their information? *martial / Juvenal*
we provided satirical perspective of info - don't know how accurate was
8 As well as needy people, who might also be clients?
people of higher rank
9 Who was the most important patron of all?
emperor
10 How did this person take part in the patronage system?
(caesarem am salutto the emperor is receiving) - callers would no longer publish
11 In what rank of society were the senators?
below the emperor - formerly leaders during Republic
12 By what three ways could men become senators?
special gift from emperor, election to quaestor positions
or through hereditary lines.

13 What privileges did senators enjoy? What did they need in order to
    be included in this group? *were purple-striped togas/special*
    seats @ public ceremonies; need 1M sesterces
14 Who were the censors? What power did they have over senators?
    magistrates- made sure senators had enough money
15 What position in society did the **equites** hold?
    equestrian class
16 In what ways would **equites** differ from senators?
    only need 400 k sesterces, not same political likely heights,
    could participate
17 What important position in government was reserved for **equites**?
    in trade
    governors
18 What two items of dress marked someone as a member of the
    equites class?
    gold ring + toga of a narrow stripe
19 Who were the plebians?
    small businessmen/craftsmen
20 What kinds of lives might they lead?
    comfortable or destitute lives
21 What help had society provided them for some time?
    distribution of free grain
22 How easy was it for plebians to rise in status?
    very hard
23 Who was Vespasian? What story about him illustrated his concern
    for the plebians? *Domitian's father - rejected labor-saving*
    device so that ples could make money.

77

Read lines 1–26 of *cēna Hateriī*, pages 241–242, and then fill in the blanks with the appropriate English word(s) to complete Haterius' invitation to his birthday party.

CENA!   CENA!   CENA!   CENA!   CENA!

You are invited to my _____ party! Come at the _____ _____ . You'll have a totally awesome time because I have a most triumphant surprise in store for you this year – and it's not acrobats jumping through hoops, either! *} 1–2*

Among my friends and clients, I have invited some ___ __ _____ (because they have lots of money) and also several _____ (who, because they are poor, want to win my favor). *} 3–5*

My guest of honor (whose favor I want to win) will be __ _____ _____ , the _____ . He will sit _____ me. I have consulted Eryllus, my arbiter elegantiae, about the seating arrangement and, in spite of his advice, __ will recline in prīmō locō. After all it is my birthday! *} 6–9*

In honor of your coming I will recline on _____ _____ , wear my _____ _____ , and even use my _____ _____ . *} 9–10*

Eryllus and I have planned a scrumptious dinner, too. For the entree, ____ _____ will bring in a huge dish laden with a _____ _____ . Then the _____ will come into the dining room to carve right before your eyes. When you see (and hear) my special stuffing – _____ _____ – you will _____ the skill of my cook. *} 11–16*

As for the wine, well, only the best _____ . And just in case you doubt my generosity, I'll have the wine steward read every label in a loud voice: "_____!" *} 16–20*

After we have supped and imbibed (a great deal), I'll snap my _____ and to the fanfare of _____ my stunning surprise entertainment will appear! *} 21–26*

Hope you can make it.
RSVP*

Quintus Haterius Latronianus

CENA!   CENA!   CENA!   CENA!   CENA!

*respondēte, sī vōbīs placet.

32.2 Deponent Verbs

Underline the correct form of the verb, and then translate the sentence.

1 postrīdiē Euphrosynē domum Hateriī iterum intrāre (cōnātus est/ cōnāta est).

2 praecō Euphrosynēn (cōnspicātus est/amplexus est); valvās nihilōminus clausit.

3 Euphrosynē servum per viam ad nāvem (regressa est/secūta est).

4 Haterius intereā cum servō Eryllō (loquēbātur/loquēbantur).

5 ubi praecō hortum (ingressus est/ingressum est), Haterius īrātissimē clāmāvit.

6 ubi praecō domō (regressus est/ēgressus est), multae lacrimae fluxērunt.

7 Eryllus philosopham quandam ab urbe Athēnīs (secūtus est/adeptus est).

8 praecō Euphrosynēn in portū (cōnspicātus est/hortātus est).

9 praecō philosophae persuādēre (cōnāta est/cōnātus est) nē discēderet.

10 effūsīs ā praecōne lacrimīs, philosopha domum Hateriī (cōnspicāta est/regressa est).

32.3 A Stoic Story

A *In **philosophia**, pages 244–245, Euphrosyne, using a common teaching technique, tells a story about a **pauper** to illustrate her philosophical belief. Throughout her story she endures many interruptions from the guests at Haterius' banquet. Write a translation for the story that Euphrosyne tells; i.e. omit all the interruptions and translate only the sections indicated by the underlining below.*

"prīmum, fābula brevis mihi nārranda est. ōlim fuit homō pauper."

"quid est pauper?" rogāvit cōnsul Sabīnus, quī mīlle servōs habēbat.

quibus verbīs audītīs, omnēs plausērunt, iocō dēlectātī. Euphrosynē autem, convīvīs tandem silentibus,

"hic pauper," inquit, "fundum parvum, uxōrem optimam, līberōs   5
cārissimōs habēbat. strēnuē in fundō labōrāre solēbat ut sibi suīsque
cibum praebēret."

"scīlicet īnsānus erat," exclāmāvit Apollōnius, quī erat homō
ignāvissimus. "nēmō nisi īnsānus labōrat."

cui respondit Euphrosynē vōce serēnā,

"omnibus autem labōrandum est. etiam eī quī spē favōris cēnās magistrātibus dant, rē vērā labōrant."

quō audītō, Haterius ērubuit; cēterī, verbīs Euphrosynēs obstupefactī, tacēbant. deinde Euphrosynē,

"pauper," inquit, "neque dīvitiās neque honōrēs cupiēbat. numquam 15 nimium edēbat nec nimium bibēbat. in omnibus vītae partibus moderātus ac temperāns esse cōnābātur."

L. Baebius Crispus senātor exclāmāvit,

"scīlicet avārus erat! nōn laudandus est nōbīs sed culpandus. Haterius noster tamen maximē laudandus est quod amīcīs sūmptuōsās cēnās 20 semper praebet."

huic Baebiī sententiae omnēs plausērunt. Haterius, plausū audītō, oblītus philosophiae servīs imperāvit ut plūs vīnī convīvīs offerrent. Euphrosynē tamen haec addidit,

"at pauper multōs cāsūs passus est. līberōs enim et uxōrem āmīsit, ubi 25 afflīxit eōs morbus gravissimus; fundum āmīsit, ubi mīlitēs eum dīripuērunt; lībertātem āmīsit, ubi ipse in servitūtem ā mīlitibus vēnditus est. nihilōminus, quia Stōicus erat, rēs adversās semper aequō animō patiēbātur; neque deōs neque hominēs dētestābātur. dēnique senectūte labōribusque cōnfectus, tranquillē mortuus est. ille 30 pauper, quem hominēs miserrimum exīstimābant, rē vērā fēlīx erat."

Haterius cachinnāns "num fēlīcem eum exīstimās," inquit, "quī tot cāsūs passus est?"

B *Now examine each interruption carefully. What point is each interruptor making or what is the philosophical point with which each interruptor disagrees?*

32.4 Abbreviations

A *Study the list, and, with the help of an English dictionary, fill the blanks with the unabbreviated Latin form of each term and then its English translation.*

		Full Form	Translation
1	A.D.	_____	_____
2	a.m. (time)	_____	_____
3	c.	_____	_____

4 e.g.   _____ _____

5 etc.   _____ _____

6 ibid.   _____ _____

7 i.e.   _____ _____

8 N. B.   _____ _____

9 non seq.   _____ _____

10 p.m. (time)   _____ _____

11 pro tem.   _____ _____

12 P.S.   _____ _____

13 viz.   _____ _____

B *Complete the following paragraphs with one of the Latin abbreviations from A.*

Quint Jolly set his alarm clock for 5:30 ____(1) because his Latin class was going to the Museum of Art and History. There was a special exhibit of artifacts from the reign of the Emperor Claudius, who died ____(2) 54 ____(3). The exhibit featured many items, ____(4) coins, jewelry, glassware, ____(5), from the period.

Quint checked to be sure he had everything he needed for the day, ____(6) bus fare, permission slip, money for lunch, and study guide for the museum. He reread the notice on the bottom of the permission slip: "Buses for the museum will leave from school promptly at 6:30. ____(7) Latecomers will be responsible for their own transportation."

As Quint's modes of transportation were human-powered, ____(8) walking, bicycling and skateboarding, and as he was acting as consul ____(9) of the Latin Club during the consul's absence, he gave himself ample time to walk to school.

Before he left, Quint left a note for his mother.

Dear Mom,

My Latin teacher, Mister Magister, said that we should return home this afternoon between 4:30 and 5:00 ____(10).

Love, Quint

____(11) If it rains, we may get home a little later.

32.5 Word Power

A *Supply a derivative of* **compōnō**, **condūcō**, **convertō**, *or* **scindō** *to complete the following sentences.*

1 A car with a removable top is called a ____ .

2 Toscanini was a renowned ____ of the NBC Symphony Orchestra.

3 The students were required to write a ____ about their summer experiences.

4 Unless your attendance improves, we shall ____ your membership.

5 Rest and a balanced diet are ____ to recovering from a serious illness.

6 The ____ from cynic to altruist is rare indeed.

7 The tailor could not cut the cloth, since he had misplaced his ____ .

8 She analyzed the contraption by looking at its various ____ .

B **-sion** *or* **-tion**? *Give a derivative from a Vocabulary Checklist word which completes the following sentences.*

1 We put an ____ onto our house. (**addere**)

2 Dictatorships survive on the ____ of the people. (**opprimere**)

3 ____ is an efficient way of transferring energy. (**condūcere**)

4 The ____ of praise heaped on the author was excessive. (**effundere**)

5 The last ____ of Christians occurred in the reign of Diocletian. (**secūtus**)

6 The environmentalists were interested in the ____ of the soil. (**compōnere**)

7 Kelley Greene did not care for her ____, nor did Sterling Silver. (**appellāre**)

8 The students hoped for ____ from the university in order to continue their studies. (**subvenīre**)

32.6 Roman Beliefs

Read pages 249–252 in your textbook and answer the following:

1 Name the temple on the Capitoline. To what three gods was this temple dedicated? What other god was honored there?
Temple of Jupiter Optimus maximus. dedicated to Jupiter, Juno, Minerva

2 What three types of divinities were worshiped by the Romans?
Greek, ever-present spirits & local deities & numius were wor.

3 What two things would define one of the "mystery religions"?
offered hope of life after death, required initiation in ceremonies

4 What two pieces of evidence show that Isis was revered, e.g., in Pompeii and Rome, at the time of our stories?
It was enlarged in Pompeii & rebuilt in Rome

5 Give two examples of Roman authorities resisting the worship of gods from outside Italy.
Mithraism & worship of Bachus/liberis

6 Who was Mithras? What were his powers? Why did the worship of Mithras appeal to many soldiers?
an ancient spirit of light that became the god of Mithraism appealing bc exalted ideas of loyalty

7 Describe the initiation into Mithraism and the **Mithraea** in which this took place.
Seven grades of initiation, involving various tests. Mithraea caves built partially underground

8 Where have **Mithraea** been found? What assumptions have been made about the kind of worshipers in these buildings?
Rome, w mediterrane and Rhine/Danube provinces, thought would app. to officers in army wealthy

9 How did the attitude of the Roman authorities towards Jews in Rome vary?
Augustus was tolerant; however Tiberius/ Claudius expelled them from the city

10 What happened to Christians in the time of Claudius (about 35 years before our stories)? Why did this happen?
They were expelled, because they were confused by the emperor w/ Jewish people

11 Why did St. Paul come to Rome? What evidence does he give of Christians in Rome at that time?
To appeal to emperor. passed on greetings from christians living in city.

12 Why could Christians sometimes be suspected of wrongdoing?
Their religion was foreign, may have involved secret rights

13 What use did Nero make of the Christians? How typical of Roman behavior towards Christians were Nero's acts?
made them scapegoats for great fire in office. not typical at all.

14 When was Christianity finally tolerated in the Roman empire?
313 CE

15 Describe Stoicism as shown in Euphrosyne's lecture at Haterius' party.
main aim should be virtue/right behavior, no pleasure

16 Who was Epictetus? Summarize two points about his teaching given in the passage.
a Greek/former slave - not to be opinionated take whatever life offers you

17 Why was it to be expected that some Stoics might get into trouble with the emperor?
Stoics tended to disapprove of one-man rule/no hereditary rule

18 List five ways temples might be used in Rome.
meeting places for senate, offices for magistrates, also religion, place w/ treatises

19 Describe five examples of **feriae** celebrated in Rome.
dances of salii in March, Parentalia in Feb, matronalia in March, vestalia in June & Saturnalia in December

dē amōre Mārtis et Veneris

The **pantomīmus** Paris performed for his lover, the Empress Domitia Augusta, on a private stage in the palace of her husband Domitian. The performance was a one-man version of the love-affair between Mars and Venus, a story of divine adultery that mirrored the actual adultery between the empress and the **pantomīmus**.

*The story below is a retelling of the myth, based on the Latin version of Ovid, in his **Metamorphoses**, IV. 169–189. When you have read this story, answer the questions that follow.*

deus Sōl prīmus adulterium Veneris et Mārtis vīdit, quod semper omnia prīmus videt. quī, magnō dolōre affectus, Vulcānō, fīliō Iūnōnis, marītōque Veneris, fūrtum atque locum fūrtī quam celerrimē dēmōnstrāvit. quae cum Vulcānus audīvisset, palluit et statuam auream, quam callidē sculpēbat, statim ōmīsit. deinde īrā commōtus, diū in   5
officīnā labōrābat; tandem, catēnīs gracilibus ex aere excūsīs, rētia perfēcit ut laqueīs subtīlibus amantēs dēprehenderet. haec rētia, quae tantā arte facta sunt ut tāctūs levēs mōmentaque parva sequerentur, Vulcānus in lectō Veneris collocāvit. postquam Venus, uxor Vulcānī, cum adulterō Mārte in lectum cōnscendit et Mārs, "venī, mea columba," exclāmāvit, in   10
mediīs amplexibus rētibus subtīlibus implicātī sunt. quōs cum vīdisset, Vulcānus cēterōs deōs arcessīvit ut flāgitium patefaceret. dī, Venerem Mārtemque cōnspicātī, valdē dērīsērunt.

fūrtum: fūrtum	here *secret love*	dēprehenderet: dēprehendere	*seize*
callidē	*cleverly*	tāctūs: tāctus	*touch*
gracilibus: gracilis	*thin, slender*	levēs: levis	*light*
aere: aes	*bronze*	mōmenta: mōmentum	*movement*
excūsīs: excūdere	*forge*	sequerentur: sequī	here *yield to*
rētia: rēte	*net* (cf. **rētiārius**)	amplexibus: amplexus	*embrace*
laqueīs: laqueus	*snare, trap*	implicātī sunt: implicāre	*entangle*
subtīlibus: subtīlis	*of fine texture*	flāgitium: flāgitium	*shame*

1 Who was the first to see the adultery? Why?
2 How did the Sun react? What did he do?
3 How did Vulcan react? What did he drop?
4 Describe the snare which Vulcan created. Where was it?
5 Describe the success of his snare.
6 What did Vulcan do when he saw Venus and Mars? Why?
7 What was the gods' reaction? How else might they have reacted?
8 If the Empress Domitia and the **pantomīmus** Paris were the real-life counterparts of Venus and Mars, who together were the real-life counterparts of Vulcan?

Be a pantomīmus!

You too can be a pantomīmus and imitate Paris imitating the dying Dido.

1   Make appropriate masks, if you wish. If you are the sole performer, you will need one mask with two painted sides, one side suitable for the male characters, Aeneas and Mercury, the other side for Dido. If you are performing this as a group, you could make three separate masks.
2   Create miming movements to accompany the story below.
3   Tape some suitable music as accompaniment, or compose and play some original music.
4   Ask other friends to read out together the following story, while you mime the actions.
5   Perform before an audience and/or make a video recording.

Dying Dido

Dido was watching Aeneas and his men on the beach, busily getting their ships ready to leave Carthage. At last Dido knew Aeneas was really leaving. There was nothing she could do or say to stop him. "You traitor!" she cried. "How dare you leave me? Does our love mean nothing to you? You're mad to put out to sea in the dead of winter. And what about me? What will happen to me?"

Crying bitterly, Dido decided to kill herself and ordered her slaves to cut wood and build a huge funeral pyre. Then she herself climbed up to the top and put there all the things in the palace which belonged to Aeneas. "I will burn all this," she said, "yes, even our marriage bed, on the day he leaves me."

On the night before Aeneas was planning to sail away, he fell asleep exhausted. Almost immediately Mercury appeared to him and warned him to sail away while he still could. After Mercury departed, Aeneas woke up and ordered the ships to sail at once.

At dawn Dido looked out from her window and saw all the Trojan ships disappearing on the northern horizon. At first she thought of sending her own ships to follow them, but the Trojans had too good a start and she knew her own fleet would never catch them now. Instead, she cursed Aeneas and all his descendants, calling on the gods to avenge her betrayal.

Crying loudly, she climbed to the top of the pyre, unsheathed a sword, and, with one, final groan, fell forward onto the blade.

What's in your future?

Cover half the page. Player A sees only the A side, and B sees only the B side.
A asks the odd-numbered questions, with B choosing and reading aloud the
correct answer, verified by A. B reads the even-numbered questions, with A
choosing and reading aloud the correct answer, verified by B.

A

1 quid accidet sī ad amphitheātrum
   ierimus?
   (quīnquāgintā gladiātōrēs
   incitābimus.)

2 flammae eum dēvorābunt.
   Tychicus eum comprehendet.

3 quid accidet nisi praecō Euphrosynēn
   invēnerit?
   (necesse erit eī domō exīre.)

4 hospitēs eam intentē audient.
   hospitēs eam ēbriī dērīdēbunt.

5 quid accidet sī coquus aprum sciderit?
   (multae avēs ēvolābunt.)

6 uxor Rūfilla semper vītam dēplōrābit.
   uxor Rūfilla eum laudābit.

7 quid accidet sī patrōnum vīsitāverō?
   (praecō tē abiget.)

8 multam pecūniam accipiam.
   domum sine pecūniā redībō.

9 quid accidet sī nullam pecūniam
   accēperō?
   (pauper manēbis.)

10 Imperātor eī sacerdōtium dabit.
    Haterius sepulcrum splendidum
    exstruet.

B

1 duodecim aurīgās vidēbimus.
   quīnquāgintā gladiātōrēs
   incitābimus.

2 quid accidet nisi Paris vitiīs suīs
   dēstiterit?
   (flammae eum dēvorābunt.)

3 necesse erit eī domum redīre.
   necesse erit eī domō exīre.

4 quid accidet sī Euphrosynē dē
   philosophiā dīxerit?
   (hospitēs eam ebriī dērīdēbunt.)

5 multae avēs ēvolābunt.
   aper miser lacrimābit.

6 quid accidet sī Salvius iter ad
   Britanniam fēcerit?
   (uxor Rūfilla semper vītam
   dēplōrābit.)

7 praecō tē abiget.
   gladiātōrēs tē interficient.

8 quid accidet sī clientēs pecūniam
   rapientēs spectāveris?
   (domum sine pecūniā redībō.)

9 dīves fiēs.
   pauper manēbis.

10 quid accidet sī Haterius agellum
    ēmerit?
    (Haterius sepulcrum splendidum
    exstruet.)

33.4 Word Power

Fill in each blank with a derivative from one of the following Latin words. The Latin words are given in the order in which they are used.

ācriter, excipere, crās, certāre, contrā, movēre, sevērus, eicere

The irate speaker's remarks were filled with ____ . He took ____ to the fact that the mayor had ____ so long to make a decision. The speaker and his supporters had made a ____ effort to rally support for his cause.

The mayor wasted no time in ____ the speaker, point by point, with genuine ____ . After heated discussion, the mayor ____ in his opinion and said that the speaker would be ____ from the proceedings if he did not moderate his remarks and behavior.

33.5 Roman Entertainment

Read pages 266–269 in your textbook and answer the following:

1 What were the **lūdī scaenicī** and the **lūdī circensēs**? How frequently were they celebrated? Give three reasons for holding them.
2 In what way did the seating at these games reflect divisions in society? Where did women sit?
3 What two forms of entertainment had largely supplanted formal plays? Give one example of an attempt to revive interest in drama by a lavish production.
4 Describe the art of the pantomime actor.
5 How did mimes differ from pantomimes?
6 Where were the **lūdī circensēs** held? Give one piece of evidence that shows how popular they were.
7 Explain the meanings of the following words as used in connection with the races: **dēfīxiōnēs**, **factiōnēs**, **mappa**, **spīna**, and **mēta**.
8 What was the usual program for a day at the races?
9 Describe the method of racing, the art of the charioteer, and the danger involved in such races.
10 Explain the words **mūnera**, **vēnātiōnēs**, and **naumachiae**.
11 How did two Romans during the Republic use elephants in **vēnātiōnēs**?
12 Describe the **mūnera** put on by Augustus. What contribution did Vespasian and Titus make to the performance of the **mūnera**?
13 When was a triumph held? Describe the triumphal procession of Vespasian and Titus.
14 What did the various forms of entertainment offer to the many people living in Rome?

Rōma ardet!

This passage tells you something about the Great Fire of Rome in A.D. 64. Read the passage through carefully and answer the questions below.

Nerōne Imperātōre, incendium maximum in urbe accidit. ortum est in eā parte urbis quā plūrimae tabernae sitae erant. quibus in tabernīs multa inerat merx.

mercātōrēs, quī in hāc regiōne habitābant, flammās cōnspicātī statim clāmōrēs sustulērunt. prīmum ipsī flammās exstinguere cōnābantur. tum 5 amīcīs et familiīs accurrentibus hamās trādidērunt in quibus aquam ferrent ut incendium exstinguerent.

cēterī autem hominēs, domibus relictīs, ex eā regiōne aufugere cōnstituērunt. sed difficile erat tantae multitūdinī ēgredī, quod viae angustae erant. paucī quidem ad loca tūta effūgērunt; multī, quia vel fessī 10 vel ignārī erant, circumventī flammīs periērunt.

cum hoc incendium urbem vexāret, Nerō diēs fēstōs prope mare agēbat. nūntiātō incendiō, in urbem quam celerrimē regressus cīvibus auxilium dedit. tantā misericordiā affectus est ut eīs, quōrum domūs dēlētae erant, hortōs suōs patefaceret. ibi aedificia subitāria exstruī iussit. 15

quīnque diēs flāgrābat incendium. flammīs sextō diē exstinctīs damnum aestimārī poterat. ex quattuordecim regiōnibus quattuor tantum manēbant integrae, trēs solō tenus dēlētae erant. in cēterīs superfuērunt pauca aedificia.

Nerōne: Nerō	*Nero*	subitāria: subitārius	*temporary*
incendium	*fire*	damnum	*loss, damage*
ortum est: orīrī	*start, arise*	aestimārī: aestimāre	*reckon, calculate*
hamās: hama	*bucket*	quattuordecim	*fourteen*
misericordiā:		integrae: integer	*unharmed*
misericordia	*pity*	solō tenus	*to ground level*

1 Where did the fire begin? Why did it spread so quickly?
2 What did the merchants do to fight the fire?
3 Why did they behave differently from everyone else?
4 Why was it difficult to escape?
5 Give two reasons why people died.
6 Why was Nero absent from Rome?
7 What measures did he take?
8 How serious was the fire?
9 Think of the ways by which an outbreak of fire is dealt with today and then discuss the difficulties which, on the evidence of this passage, the Romans experienced in a similar situation.

88

34.2 Word Power

A *Complete the following analogies:*

1 nunc : iam : : nōn : _____
2 ad : ab : : prope : _____
3 iubeō : mandō : : obscūritās : _____
4 turba : multitūdō : : signum : _____
5 dīcit : inquit : : redīre : _____

B *Copy the following words. Put parentheses around the Latin root from this Stage contained inside these derivatives; give the Latin word and its meaning from which the derivative comes.*

For example: conservation con(serva)tion servare – to save

1 exhortation
2 concomitant
3 deprecate
4 compendium
5 imminent
6 condemnation
7 irreversible

34.3 Progressions

Fill in the blanks with words which properly complete the progression:

1 opus, _____ , operī, _____ , opere

2 pauper, pauperior, _____

3 _____ , equitēs, _____ , imperātor

4 heri, hodiē, _____

5 prīmus, tertius, _____ , septimus, _____

6 nascī, vīvere, _____

7 eram, sum, _____

8 morior, morī, _____

9 Chrȳsogonus, Haterius, _____ , Domitiānus

10 difficile, difficilius, _____

Once you have read this story on pages 279–280 of your textbook, write out the Latin phrase or sentence which correctly describes the action in each picture.

a) Paris conspicatur

mater militibus praetendins
porta erat

b) cum quasi fugiens retro in hortum cucurrit

ipse ..... ostendit

c) ecce Paris! Paris effugere conatur!

statim militbus clamaverunt

d) Paris per hortum modo huc modo illuc ruebat

modo huc   modo illuc

hunc prosilire

e) simulacque intraverunt

milites hortum laudan Paris consundit

f) intectum conarus est

g) sed tegulae tectum labricae erunt

91

Who had Paris killed?   A ROMAN 'WHODUNIT"

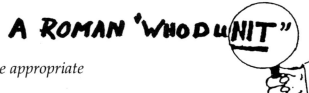

*Fill in the detective's logbook by writing the appropriate
Latin description in each box.*

Latin Descriptions
- uxor Imperātōris quae multum amāvit Paridem
- cum amīcō Epaphrodītō clam locūtus est
- Salvius tribūnum mīlitum praetōriānōrum caput Paridis amputāre iussit
- Paride Domitiāque domum Hateriī vacuam invītātīs, mīlitēs praetōriānōs illūc mīsit quī eōs caperent
- Epaphrodītus Imperātōrī persuāsit ut uxōrem suam Domitiam ex Ītaliā relēgāret
- ā Paride ac Domitiā ēlūsus est
- Imperātōrī persuāsit ut Salviō cōnsulātum prōmitteret
- pantomīmus quī Domitiae fābulam in aulae Domitiānī ātriō ēgit

LOGBOOK
Conspiracy in the Imperial Palace

Suspects in Crime

Gāius Salvius Līberālis	Tiberius Claudius Epaphrodītus

Crimes

homicīdium	relēgātiō iniusta

Criminal Charges

īnsidiās parāvit	praemium prōmīsit

Victims

Paris	Domitia Augusta

Freedmen and Freedwomen

Read pages 286–290 in your textbook and answer the following:

1 What was very unusual about the status of freedmen in Roman society? *They were given Roman citizenship after freedom*

2 In what way was a freedman's name changed when the person was freed? *He had 3 names, two of which were inherited from the ex master*

3 List four privileges the freedman now enjoyed. *voting, business agreements, marriage,*

4 What limitations were there for a freedman? What was a freedwoman not allowed to do? *They could not be senators/equites, freedwoman couldn't become slavery. buy off life out of senators wife*

5 What five obligations might a **cliens** be expected to fulfill for his **patrōnus**? *leave money to patron in will, protect them from harm + help them a certain # days/year*

6 List five things a **patrōnus** might do for his **cliens**. *help client w/ sportula + salutatio, pay for decent funeral, guardian of cliens children*

7 Describe Pliny's treatment of his freedman Zosimus. What do these details suggest about this particular patron–client relationship? *kind + affectionate/arranged a holiday when z had funding for new life, help to client if had no job*

8 What evidence about freedmen and freedwomen do the four tombstones cited in the passage give? *Set up tombstones to honor their master + vice versa, freed people buried w/ job*

9 In what basic financial way would freeing a slave benefit the owner? *No longer would have to pay for slave's amenities, the master + ex master might marry freed woman*

10 List crafts or skills that freedmen might have. *teacher, musician, accounting, trading, bank work, secretary*

11 Why did some freedmen enjoy substantial success? *Filled important managerial positions, wealth [secretary]*

12 Describe two examples of very successful freedmen, one pair from Pompeii, and an individual from literature. *Vettii brothers set up own business in Pompeii + Trimalchio (Satyrica)*

13 Nevertheless, what disadvantages might a freedman suffer? *Prejudice viewed as social inferiors by freeborn*

14 What contrasting views on the attitudes of a **patrōnus** do Juvenal and Pliny give? *Juvenal - clients get the bad food / treated badly + Pliny - makes sure guests are treated right*

15 What social success of Horace did people envy? *his friendship w/ Maecenas a patron of arts*

16 In what way did Horace praise both his father and Maecenas, his patron? *intellectually + moral training → social fairness Father gave*

17 What special privilege did only freedmen enjoy? *one the three priests (seviri Augustales)*

18 Explain the terms **seviri Caesaris** and **libertī Augustī**. *→ slave name ← freedman liberti A Augusti*

19 Explain the terms **ā libellīs**, **ab epistulīs**, and **ā ratiōnibus**. What position did Epaphroditus hold? *a libellis - secretary, ab epistulis - correspondence, a rationibus - accountant freedwomen*

20 Who was Pallas? How had he been rewarded? *secretary a rationibus of Emperor Claudius - won honorary praetorship*

21 Describe Pliny's reaction to the inscription recording Pallas' honors. *He was furious, because he thought Pallas was insulting the praetorian rank, for refusing the money*

[left margin notes:]
couldn't not serve in army, be an electoral candidate

show respect, attend him in public, mutual helpfulness

well well deserved

a libellis - secretary rationibus - accounts, slaves secretary, a libellis

34.7 Which is the missing principal part of the verb?

Write the missing principal part of each verb in the appropriate squares of the puzzle. The numerals in the parentheses at the end of each clue refer to the number of the Stage Vocabulary Checklist where the principal parts will be found.

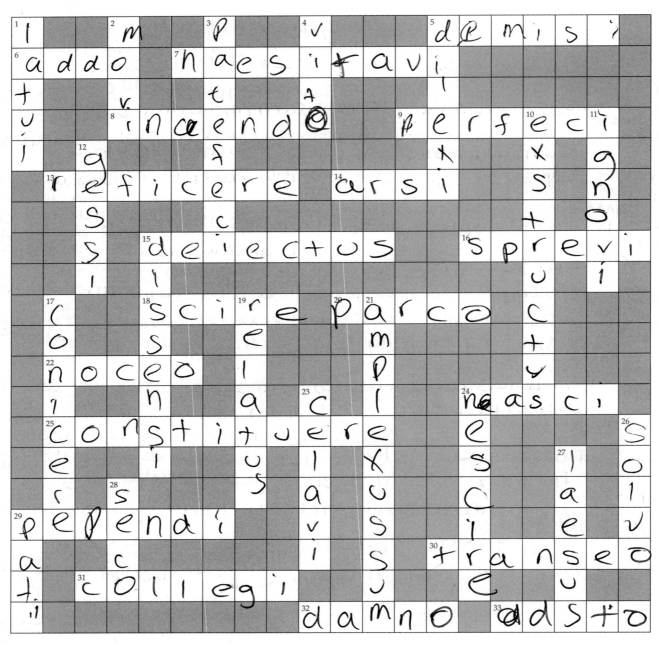

ACROSS

5 dēmittō, dēmittere, _____, dēmissus *let down, lower* (30)

16 _____, addere, addidī, additus *add* (32)

7 haesitō, haesitāre, _____, *hesitate* (25)

8 _____, incendere, incendī, incēnsus *burn, set fire to* (27)

9 perficiō, perficere, _____, perfectus *finish* (29)

13 reficiō, _____, refēcī, refectus *repair* (31)

14 ardeō, ardēre, _____ *burn, be on fire* (27)

15 dēiciō, dēicere, dēiēcī, _____ *throw down* (21)

16 spernō, spernere, _____, sprētus *despise, reject* (29)

18 sciō, _____, scīvī *know* (23)

20 _____, parcere, pepercī *spare* (22)

22 _____, nocēre, nocuī *hurt* (27)

24 nāscor, _____, nātus sum *be born* (34)

25 cōnstituō, _____, cōnstituī, cōnstitūtus *decide* (28)

29 pendeō, pendēre, _____ *hang*

30 _____, trānsīre, trānsiī *cross* (24)

31 colligō, colligere, _____, collēctus *gather, collect* (26)

32 _____, damnāre, damnāvī, damnātus *condemn* (34)

33 _____, adstāre, adstitī *stand by*

DOWN

1 lateō, latēre, _____ *lie hidden* (25)

2 moveō, movēre, _____, mōtus *move* (33)

3 patefaciō, patefacere, _____, patefactus *reveal* (24)

4 _____, vītāre, vītāvī, vītātus *avoid* (22)

5 dīligō, dīligere, _____, dīlēctus *be fond of* (28)

10 exstruō, exstruere, exstrūxī, _____ *build* (30)

11 ignōscō, ignōscere, _____ *forgive* (32)

12 gerō, gerere, _____, gestus *wear* (23)

15 dissentiō, dissentīre, _____ *disagree* (22)

17 coniciō, _____, coniēcī, coniectus *hurl, throw* (33)

19 referō, referre, rettulī, _____ *bring back* (26)

21 amplector, amplectī, _____ _____ *embrace* (34)

23 cēlō, cēlāre, _____, cēlātus *hide* (21)

24 nesciō, _____, nescīvī *not know* (25)

26 _____, solvere, solvī, solūtus *loosen, untie* (28)

27 laedō, laedere, laesī, _____ *harm* (25)

28 _____, secāre, secuī, sectus *cut* (31)

29 patior, _____, passus sum *suffer* (34)

Who was Paris?

The poet Martial had to wait until after Domitian's death to write the poem on Paris, quoted below. The poem shows how very much the actor was admired. The epitaph is no ordinary eulogy: according to Martial, all the arts died with Paris.

A *After reading the Martial poem below, read the following translations:*

quisquis Flāminiam teris, viātor,
nōlī nōbile praeterīre marmor.
urbis dēliciae salēsque Nīlī,
ars et grātia, lūsus et voluptās,
Rōmānī decus et dolor theātrī
atque omnēs Venerēs Cupīdinēsque
hōc sunt condita, quō Paris, sepulcrō.

O traveler, faring north from Rome,
Do not pass by this noble tomb.
The city's joy, the wit of Nile,
Pleasure, delight, and art, and style,
The pride and glory of our age,
The sorrows of the Roman stage
And all the charms the Loves devise
Lie in this tomb where Paris lies.

Rolfe Humphries

Traveler on the Flaminian Way,
Pause a little here, and stay
On this monument your eyes–
Here the actor, Paris, lies,
Delight of Rome, the wit of Nile,
All joy, all art, all grace, all style,
Of all the Roman theater chief,
Its former joy and now its grief;
Nor for him only shed your tear–
Love and desire lie with him here.

Olive Pitt-Kethley

Traveler who trudge the Flaminian way, do not pass by this noble marble tomb. The City's delight, and Egypt's wit, art and gracefulness, jest and merriment, the glory and grief of the Roman stage, and all the Venuses and Cupids, are buried in this tomb with Paris.

N. M. Kay

B *Which version of the translations do you think most closely captures the spirit of the original? Explain why you think so.*

C *Write an English version yourself.*